D1480664

The Black Preacher
in America

JUN 31.73

2

142929   230
                                        Ha

Hamilton
Black preacher in America

MEDIA SERVICES
EVANSTON TOWNSHIP HIGH SCHOOL
EVANSTON, ILLINOIS 60204

Date Due

 23-236 PRINTED IN U.S.A.

The
Black
Preacher
in
America

Charles V. Hamilton

William Morrow & Company, Inc.
New York 1972

MEDIA SERVICES
EVANSTON TOWNSHIP HIGH SCHOOL
EVANSTON, ILLINOIS 60204

Copyright © 1972 by Charles V. Hamilton

All rights reserved. No part of this book may be reproduced or
utilized in any form or by any means, electronic or mechanical,
including photocopying, recording or by any information storage
and retrieval system, without permission in writing from the
Publisher. Inquiries should be addressed to William Morrow and
Company, Inc., 105 Madison Ave., New York, N.Y. 10016.

Printed in the United States of America.

Hamilton, Charles V
    The Black preacher in America.

    Includes bibliographical references.
    1. Negro clergy—United States. I. Title.
BR563.N4H34   253   78-170231
ISBN 0-688-00006-1
ISBN 0-688-05006-9 (pbk.)

230
Ha

7.95

10/3/78

To Dona

142929 √

Contents

The Black Preacher
in America

Author to Reader

This book is about a figure who has been, and remains, one of the most praised and most condemned persons in American society: the black preacher. Comments about him run the spectrum from "jackleg" to hustler to statesman to "man of God," and include virtually every conceivable indictment and award society has to offer. He is without question, the one spokesman for his people with the longest tenure of leadership, dating back to the moment black people were brought to this country as indentured servants and slaves. There is no "typical" black preacher, and this book does not attempt to create one. What it does is to discuss, historically and currently, several aspects of his life, with particular emphasis on his many roles in the black church and in the black communities.

The black preacher has been an important person in the lives of black people, and this book examines some of the fundamental ways he has and the reasons why this is so.

As a black man, I find it most difficult, if not impossible, to deal dispassionately with this subject. Like so many blacks, I grew up in the black Baptist church and was immensely impressed by Reverend William Johnson of Greater St. John Baptist Church on the South Side of Chicago. Many of us were influenced in the 1940's by this obviously intelligent man who stood in the pulpit every Sunday and spoke words of wisdom, and who had the respect of our parents and aunts and uncles and neighbors. As I recall, we were not much moved by the substance of what he had to say—after all, we took most of that for granted: the existence of God, that we had to live honestly and righteously if we wanted to go to heaven when we died, that God would punish us if we strayed from the straight and narrow path, and, of course, that we had to be "born again," that is, baptized, if we were to be "saved." Religious doctrine became considerably more complicated for some of us later on. But at that time, in those younger years, a lot of things were much simpler, and one's fundamental religious belief was one of them.

Ours was "the friendly church by the library" (at 48th and Michigan Boulevard, next to the all-black-staffed public library), and when we were old enough, we sought eagerly to join the junior usher board or the junior choir, or do whatever else was sure to elicit approval from Reverend Johnson, which meant, of course, approval from our parents as well. Not to mention approval from God. I remember wanting to be a preacher like Reverend Johnson. And this was largely because of the impression he made on me as a leader, as one who was articulate, educated and highly respected. He was one of the few black men we knew who wore a suit during the week! And he had a nice apartment in a very well-kept building, not just a one- or two-room kitchenette with shared kitchen and bath facilities. Like the few postal workers, men who "ran on the road" (Pullman porters) and the handful of black teachers, he was not "on relief." All these things, I, and many of my regular Sunday-school classmates, admired and wanted, and Reverend Johnson was one of the best models we had. When he talked, grown-ups listened, and it was clear that he spoke with authority and commanded respect. Men said "Excuse me, Reverend" when they cursed in his presence in the barbershops, and they frequently called on him to provide that final, definitive voice that could settle an argument or decide a dispute (though not arguments over sports, of course).

If it is not easy to discuss this subject dispassionately, neither is it really necessary to do so. The black preacher is, for the most part, a passionate figure in the lives of black people. He intends to be; his people want him to be; and it would be straining to achieve almost an unnatural condition to make it otherwise. Those two- to two-and-a-half-hour Sunday-morning services at Greater St. John were periods of intense emotionalism. In our church, there was soul-stirring music from two choirs (the senior choir and the gospel choir); there were at least two moving prayers from a deacon, a visiting minister or an associate minister of the church; and these were highlighted by a strong sermon, never less than fifty minutes or an hour, punctuated with a great deal of "talk-back" and frequent shouting. One was not supposed to be emotionless, or to try to suppress one's feelings. Of course, the more restrained worshipers did not shout or talk back—a quiet nod or hum or lifting of the hand would do—but to remain untouched meant it was not a particularly successful service.

As preteens in the early 1940's, I and my friends in the church did not know the politics of our pastor. We often heard our parents, relatives and church elders describe him vaguely, and admiringly, as a "race man," but this simply meant that he was for equal rights for the "colored people." I remember his talking patriotism at the beginning of World War II, but there were no long, open discussions in the church, at least none that filtered down to us youngsters, about racial protests or even rights of citizenship. Again, some of us took it for granted that Negroes deserved to be treated like all other citizens, and that things were very bad in the South and that segregation was wrong.

When my older brother went into the Army, he joined a group of other young men from the church whose names were put on a bulletin board in the church lobby, and Reverend Johnson and our Sunday-school teacher always reminded us to write our "V" letters that week. If politicians came to our church to speak about politics or elections, we youngsters did not feel the impact of what they had to say, and there is no reason to deny that we probably really did not listen or care. We looked forward to the singing and preaching, and little else. Probably everyone in the church then was strongly pro-Franklin D. Roosevelt, and local electoral politics was not a part of the religious menu we were served.

Those were the beginning days of the "racial breakthroughs" and the "Negro firsts." I recall Reverend Johnson's proudly announcing that one young lady on the usher board had been hired by the telephone company; another man, a deacon or trustee of the church, I think, had been hired as one of the first motormen on the city's streetcars. These things made Reverend Johnson and the all-black congregation proud, and he invariably wove them into his sermons: how God will make a way if you just trust in Him; how the Lord helps those who help themselves; and how the Lord does not intend for any people to be "held down" and abused for too long.

So it was easy to identify with Reverend Johnson and to want to be like him. And I bring that background and cultural experience to the writing of this book, with no strained pretense at dispassionate observation of the subject matter.

Neither did we believe that all preachers were like our Reverend Johnson. Occasionally we heard whispers about how some other minister in another church was "playing around" with some of the women in the church, or how a particular minister was pocketing a large part of the weekly collection (we always had at least three collections each Sunday morning). We never drew any general conclusions about these rumors or facts—that is, they always applied to some other minister, and we *knew* that Reverend Johnson would never act like that. "It takes all kinds to make a world," our parents would say. "And the Lord will take care of the wrongdoers in due time." To us, *our* Reverend Johnson was a man of high moral character, and it would have been virtually impossible to convince us otherwise. It was, in fact, his image of having strong moral values that impressed us.

This book is not concerned primarily with the church as an institution. Its focus is on the preacher. But as it will be seen, most frequently when one is talking about the black preacher, one is talking about the black church. Very often the two are inseparable for analytical purposes. But my main concern is the preacher, as an individual who fills a pulpit, who leads a congregation, who plays many roles in the community.

The first six chapters deal with the preacher's roles and activities in connection with several major topics.

Chapter I pinpoints four major themes highlighting the black preacher's relationship to black people. The emphasis here is on the black cultural context out of which this relationship comes and which must be understood in order to grasp fully the significance of this individual, whether he is a rural Alabama preacher with a congregation of less than fifty members, a Northern urban pastor of a church with more than several thousand members, a black Catholic priest or a Harlem storefront pastor.

Chapter II discusses the roles of the minister during slavery. There are many generalizations, of course, about the role of the church in black history, especially pre-Civil War: that religion was basically "otherworldly," that the minister was an agent of white oppression, that the minister was an overt or latent Nat Turner ready and willing to lead his people in open, violent revolt. This chapter reviews the different roles black preachers played during that period.

Chapter III is a presentation of the number and distribution of black preachers and churches. These data are the best available, but in discussing the black religious experience in American society, absolutely firm statistics are both hard to obtain and not particularly reliable. Many churches and preachers, because of their small congregations, simply are not included in official counts.

Chapter IV deals with the many problems involved with educating black preachers, as well as with an account of the role ministers have played in the education of black people. This is an area in which the black preacher has been quite active, but it is also one in which the profession has experienced some of its most serious weaknesses. On the whole, the group is not well educated, and this is the cause of a number of problems and criticisms.

Chapter V discusses several aspects of politics and the preacher's relationship to this field. Many ministers are not politically active; they confine their activities almost exclusively to religious matters, operating in the pulpit. For this, they are often severely criticized by others, usually younger people, who insist that the black ministry has an obligation to engage in political activism. This chapter examines the various ways black preachers act politically. It also looks at the new religiopolitical philosophy of a rapidly growing group of new Black Theologians.

Some of the most bitter fights in the black community have centered around black preachers. Chapter VI presents some of those conflicts as they have involved personalities, property and positions of power within the church. This chapter also discusses four major areas of criticism of the black ministry from various sources within the black community. Specifically, the criticisms are charges that the ministry is materialistic, nonintellectual, authoritarian and politically uninvolved. Many of the criticisms are not without substantial justification.

Chapters VII through X deal with material taken from extensive interviews with preachers around the country. Chapter VII discusses problems some ministers have with their congregations when the ministers attempt to assume roles in the church or in the community with which the parishioners do not agree. Chapter VIII examines some different experiences ministers have had in becoming trained for their profession. In Chapter IX, the highly individualistic character of some ministers is discussed. The important relationship between young people, the ministry and the church is explored in Chapter X.

As stated earlier, no effort has been made to select what may be considered typical preachers to fit preconceived categories. The only criteria for selection were the rather obvious ones: region (North and South); denomination (seven denominations are represented); demography (rural or urban); education; size of congregation. These men do not want to be considered typical of their denomination or of other colleagues in the ministry, and I have not chosen or presented them as such. Rather, here are eight black preachers talking freely about their perceptions of their work, their backgrounds, their aspirations, what prompted them to pursue the ministry, their attitudes on a variety of subjects, religious and otherwise. Thus, these chapters can only present some pictures, not the *total* picture of the black ministry. The words of these preachers tell *their* story, and I am aware that there are many more to tell. But the discussions reported here delve into many areas and problems certainly not entirely exclusive to the individual interviewee. These ministers raise issues from their vantage points, which are not solely applicable to them. Their discussions present the reader with a range of problems and a variety of solutions. While the interviewees themselves would be the first to realize that one man's solution might not apply any other place, it is possible to see some common elements of approach, analysis and insight.

When I started this venture, there was no dearth of advice from black friends who insisted that I be sure to talk to their pastor or to a certain minister whom they knew to be just the one who could provide the insights I needed. (One will find that many black people can be quite arrogant about the qualities of their own particular minister.) Each person insisted that his minister was typical in many ways and yet unique, but above all had great knowledge about the profession. This was not too far wrong about the more than forty I talked to over a period of two years. More than a few ministers admonished me to be careful about "how you generalize," and at the same time many agreed that there were common characteristics shared by very many black preachers. One man suggested that I would find that many were "born actors or teachers." "Watch what I tell you," he said. "You can just see it in that pulpit. They love to teach or they love to perform, and sometimes both." I found this to be true in many cases. The preacher is, in fact, a teacher, and if he is also a powerful orator, as many are, he combines his talents to present what can only be described as a major stage production. Indeed, one of the men interviewed noted that the black preacher served at one time as the James Brown of the black community. He presented a show, provided entertainment and received top billing in a cast that has enjoyed the longest run of any production ever put on in the American black community. But this was just part of his function, albeit an important one. There are several other functions that this book attempts to relate.

I do not deal with such people as Father Divine and the "prophets," who have built large followings and amassed fortunes; and the omission is quite deliberate. While exceedingly important, these religious ventures are largely socioreligious movements that require (and in some cases, have received) extended, exclusive research treatment. I preferred to focus primarily on the black preacher who is less prominent, less well-known. It is this person who has not received too much attention in the published literature. I wanted to confine the book to those ministers who are not perceived as God, prophets or direct messengers from God by their followers, but rather those who are seen as mortals. Some obviously are national figures with wide influence, but they are not seen as possessing divine or supernatural powers. In addition, I have not concentrated on the small cults that exist in the black religious community. These, too, are important, but they can best be dealt with separately. Indeed, there have already been some studies of these cults. My concern, then, has been with (if a generalization of a sort is permitted) the "middle minister," not the socioreligious, mass-movement type with "God qualities," nor with the leader of small cults. My judgment is that it is this middle minister who has provided the most sustained religious leadership in the black community, and who has built the largest continuing institution of the black people. He is, for that primary reason, my subject in this book.

The interviews were taped and no formal questionnaire was used. Most of the interviews lasted a minimum of two or three hours, with some consuming the greater part of four or five hours during the day. I am very grateful to

Shirley Ostholm, a graduate student at Columbia University, for her extensive interview with Father Donald Clark in Detroit, whom she had known previously, Mr. James Hopkins of Tuskegee, Alabama, one of the new black elected officials in that state (he is the first black Circuit Court Clerk in Macon County), was exceedingly helpful in putting me in contact with ministers in rural Alabama. I greatly appreciate his help. I also benefited from many discussions with my colleague at Columbia University, Professor Elliott P. Skinner. His insights as a social scientist helped me sharpen some of my own ideas. Christopher F. Edley, Sr., was helpful in suggesting particular areas to examine, especially in reference to material in Chapter VI. Hillel Black, my editor, was invaluable in pinpointing important items connected with the drafting and redrafting of the manuscript and in suggesting additional matters to develop. And, of course, this does not begin to express my appreciation for his patience.

In all cases, the ministers consented to the use of their real names rather than pseudonyms. Both the preachers and I feel that for these kinds of narratives, this adds to the authenticity of the material for the reader and is much better than the cryptic "Rev. X" or "Rev. John Doe" approach used in some social-science research and journalistic reporting.

Needless to say, I am more than grateful to all of them for their time, knowledge and candor. And if they should ask, as in the frequent preaching style of Reverend Johnson, "Have I got a witness?" they can expect from me a variety of responses frequently forthcoming from an appreciative and attentive pew:

"Well, all right!"

"Preach!"

"Go 'head on."

I

The Preacher and His People

Many Tasks to Perform, Many Roles to Play

In November, 1969, a young black man won the councilmanic seat in central Harlem on the Liberal-party ticket. It was an unusual victory in many ways, but most importantly because the black Fifth District traditionally voted for the Democratic candidate, not for the Liberal or Republican candidate. This year, however, the Democratic party had a man leading the ticket for mayor, Mario Procaccino, who was looked upon as too conservative and as a "law and order" candidate (meaning, of course, against mass black protests). The black candidate on the Democratic ticket, Jesse Gray, was a popular civil-rights leader with a long history of leading rent strikes against exploitative landlords in Harlem. But Gray was saddled with an unfortunate figure at the top of the ticket, and they both lost. Charles Taylor won, campaigning on the slogan "A vote for Taylor is a vote for Lindsay." John Lindsay, considered to be far more progressive than either the Democratic or Republican candidates, had lost his Republican primary fight for mayor the previous June to a staunch conservative, so Lindsay, the incumbent mayor, had to run on the Liberal-party ticket.

A few days after the November election, Taylor called a small meeting in his storefront headquarters in Harlem. He wanted to put together some sort of local community councils that would draw up a set of programs for him to advocate in the City Council. His plan was to have several community meetings in different parts of Harlem, and he wanted these meetings well attended with people who would actively participate. He also wanted more than the regular politicians; he wanted the "regular people." His advisors, all knowledgeable in local Harlem politics and community affairs, immediately advised him: "Get to the ministers."

The first order of business was compiling a list of names of local Harlem preachers. Other groups—young and old, militant and moderate, small and large—would be included. But the first and most unanimous suggestion was: "Get to the ministers."

And so it has been throughout the history of black people in America. The black preacher has been called upon by politicians, parishioners, peacemakers and all others. He has been a natural leader in the black community. He has a fixed base, the church; he has a perpetual constituency, the congregation, which he sees assembled for at least one to two hours each week. And he is highly respected among that constituency. If one includes the several meetings with the various church groups—deacon board, trustee board, choirs, various auxiliary clubs—that occur during the week, then the preacher's contact far exceeds one or two hours. In addition, there is the contact he has with individual members of the church on visits to their homes and in hospitals, at weddings, funerals and innumerable other special occasions. When family and friends visit from out of town, it is considered a special treat to have the minister and his family over for dinner.

He is a kind of celebrity, and his presence adds prestige to the family and the occasion. Thus the preacher has access to everyday folk on many levels in many different ways. He asks very little in the way of obligation: church attendance and dues, when you can and what you can. In fact, on balance, he is perceived by his followers as the one person in the community who gives far more than he receives.

In earlier times, especially during the nineteenth century and for most years prior to the 1930's and the New Deal, it was quite understandable that the black preacher, as leader of the black church, would be a pivotal figure. The church was pretty much unrivaled in the black community as the major institution of black folk. There were no labor unions; there were few other social, political or economic agencies in the black community among the lower class. Thus the church was the center. This situation persisted much longer in the South—particularly the rural South—than in the North, because racial segregation was more open in the South. Life was more overtly prescribed. But it was also true of the teeming Northern urban ghettos. If black people wanted to meet, the only available meeting place large enough to hold more than a handful was the church building. In addition, the church was usually centrally located, and blacks had a habit of going there, stopping off to pick up friends and neighbors. There were no lodge halls, no union halls, no school auditoriums, no community centers. They could meet at Big Bethel or at Tabernacle, and if further directions or identification was needed, which was seldom the case, "That's Reverend Jones's church," or "Where Reverend Smith pastors."

And Reverend Jones or Reverend Smith would be there to open the church, and he would usually begin the meeting with a prayer and some welcoming remarks. These comments invariably mentioned how concerned his church was for *all* the people and their problems, not just its own members. This was in part a plug, a kind of commercial, and the particular church gained added prestige in the community.

Out of this environment came the natural leadership of the black preacher. His position always propelled him up front. He was always given a seat on the platform. He was sought after by whites who wanted to reach the black community, either to receive or to give information. The black preacher was the natural, most convenient funnel. Blacks knew this, and they would, more frequently than not, turn to their ministers to intercede for them with the white Establishment. He was the most sought-after person as a character witness in court for one of his parishioners.

Consequently, at the turn of the century, W. E. B. Du Bois could write:

> The preacher is the most unique personality developed by the Negro on American soil. A leader, a politician, an orator, a "boss," an intriguer, an idealist, —all these he is, and ever, too, the centre of a group of men, now twenty, now a thousand in number. The combination of a certain adroitness with deep-seated earnestness, of tact with consummate ability, gave him his preeminence, and helps him maintain it. The type, of course, varies according to time and place, from the West Indies in the sixteenth century to New England in the nineteenth, and from the Mississippi bottoms to cities like New Orleans or New York.[1]

Blacks needed so much in the way of day-to-day necessities for survival, and leadership skills were in short supply. Carter G. Woodson noted this in his seminal study, *The History of the Negro Church:*

> There were during the Reconstruction period, moreover, so many necessities with which the Negroes had

to be supplied that the Negro preacher, often the only
one in their community sufficiently well grounded in
the fundamentals to lead them, had to devote his time
not only to church work but to every matter of concern
to the race.[2]

Another factor has broadened the preacher's contact
beyond the traditional pulpit duties. Historically and currently, in a number of instances, North and South, the
black preacher's congregation is so small and so economically poor that it cannot adequately support him and his
family. This means that he often has to seek outside employment. At times this has involved taking the church
into various economic ventures. But he is always looked
upon as "Reverend." Some ministers have combined their
ministry with barbering, which makes them exceptionally
available as the center of community activity. Indeed,
what the Catholic Church and the saloon have been traditionally to Irish-Americans,[3] the church (either Baptist or
Methodist) and the barbershop have been to black Americans. In the latter instance, there is the added impact of
having only one person serve as leader (proprietor) in both
situations.

Certainly, one plausible explanation of the early prominence of the role of the preacher stems from the fact that
blacks have been rigidly segregated in this society, and the
church has been the major black institution in a segregated society. The minister, then, has been the beneficiary
of this condition in terms of relatively unrivaled leadership. One line of argument suggests that as the walls of
racial segregation are brought down, and as blacks develop
more secular institutions, the influence of the church and
of preachers will decline. In other words, the church and
the ministry will not be the exclusive areas to which blacks
will turn for help. Other agencies will be present: unions,
fraternal organizations, social clubs with clubhouses and

social parties and dances. And some of these will be racially integrated. New black leaders will develop in these other arenas, with different bases of power.

This is undoubtedly true, and a number of writers have commented on this potential challenge to the leadership of the black church and the black preacher. Unless the black preachers change and adapt to the times, they will find that they have been surpassed altogether in their traditional multirole leadership. The president of the Inter-denominational Theological Center (predominantly black) in Atlanta, Georgia, Harry V. Richardson, made the following observation in 1966:

> As studies show, in Negro communities there are few church-sponsored programs for guidance of the young, for adult education, for health and cultural improvement or for help in occupational skills and placement. These are the kinds of services that will lead the people into a more abundant life.[4]

There are innumerable black preachers around the country engaged in the kinds of newly adaptable activities Dr. Richardson calls for. Some are described throughout this book and interviewed for this study and presented in Chapters VII through X. It is equally true that many ministers do not understand their role as one of involvement in civic matters, and they are supported in this view by their congregations. In the latter instance, one finds the average age of the congregation to be beyond forty or forty-five, with no indication that the church is able to attract an appreciable number of younger people. In a survey conducted among five hundred black college-student activists (those students who organized and participated in black student organizations on college campuses in the North and South, in both white and black colleges, between 1967 and 1971), the results showed that 85 percent indicated that they grew up in families that professed a religion. But 76 percent of the respondents also indicated that they did not now profess a religion themselves.[5] Interviews with some of these black students revealed that they were generally disappointed with what they perceived to be the "traditional black preacher who simply preaches about heaven and doesn't get involved in daily problems of black people here on earth." These students were aware of the social action of Martin Luther King, Jr., and of other black ministers such as Reverend Jesse Jackson, Reverend Albert Cleage and Malcolm X. They identified with these men, but, importantly, more as political activists than as ministers.

Some ministers will reduce their various roles, become "pulpit preachers" and accept the fact that their traditional task of being spokesmen on a number of issues is being taken over by newer leaders coming up from newer, more secular organizations. In this dynamic period, such preachers can survive for a time. They still have their congregations, albeit aging ones, and they are still sought after by those who want to reach a certain stratum of the black community. In addition, they know that many of the secular leaders are part of predominantly white structures—for example, labor unions and political parties—and are circumscribed by this association. The black church remains, then, one of the few quite independent black institutions with a black head and a black body. The Harlem political situation described at the beginning of this chapter developed precisely because Jesse Gray was on the Democratic ticket with a white leader who was unacceptable to the majority of Harlem voters. Gray's chances, in other words, were hindered by his association with the larger political party. Even Charles Taylor, the successful Liberal-party candidate, did not receive the full support of his party. He indicated that he had to rely heavily on local, indigenous groups, many of them churches. Thus, while his Liberal-party affiliation was a definite advantage in *that* election, it could not be considered a strong, independent base on which to build political power. Until predominantly or exclusively black secular-political institutions develop to provide effective leadership in the black communities, one can expect the black preachers to continue to be sought after as important and influential figures beyond matters related solely to the pulpit.

Thus, the black preacher definitely will find that he will be required less and less to assume multileadership roles. But as long as he is the leader of a viable all-black institution—whether overtly politicized or not—he will be able to exercise influence precisely because of the exclusivity of that institution. Newer black leaders who emerge as subagents of larger, extracommunity organizations will indeed be able to assume many of the leadership functions previously performed almost totally by the black preachers. But for the next several years, if not decades, it is wise to assume that many more meetings will be held by these secular leaders, black and white, who will strongly advise: "Get to the ministers."

Finally, it is far more likely that the black ministry will continue to play an important role in the lives of lower-class blacks than with the upwardly mobile black middle class. It is in the growing, but still relatively small, latter group that one finds blacks moving out into other spheres of activity, finding them turning less to their preacher for help. But literally millions of lower-class black people will continue to look to their own black communities and organizations, most notably the churches, for social and political, if not always economic, leadership. And it is in this instance, again, that the black ministry will continue to be a crucial focal point for guidance and leadership.

"My Pastor"

One seldom hears lower-class black people speak of "my lawyer" or of "my doctor" or even "my country." These terms do not appear with any degree of frequency in normal conversations on the use of professional services or in discussions relating to citizenship, nationality or patriotism. Certainly blacks use lawyers and doctors, but they do not have the kind of regular relationship that gives rise to a feeling of mutual, personal commitment. They go to a doctor, and he treats them; they go to a lawyer, and he handles their case; but that is the extent of the relationship. It is almost purely business. Blacks pay their taxes and fight in wars in the country's military service, but it is out of obligation and duty, not out of a sense of "my country, right or wrong, my country."

But a discussion of religion among church-affiliated blacks will frequently include the phrase "my pastor." And when the phrase is used, there is a strong sense of mutual, personal attachment. The speaker will quote his pastor, cite him authoritatively, tell what his pastor has done for him, what the pastor said in his sermon last Sunday. There is a feeling of trust and mutual loyalty not found in other relationships.

Drake and Cayton [6] described frequent complaints against preachers and churches heard on Chicago's South Side during their study of Bronzeville: Church is a "racket"; ministers don't practice what they preach; preachers are hustlers and pimps. These are still rather widespread feelings, but, interestingly enough, a particular church-affiliated person will not consider these complaints to be true about *his* minister. He does not believe that *his* pastor is a racketeer or a pimp; maybe this is the case with the minister up the street or in the next block, but not "my pastor." Thus, the preacher needs sanction only from his *own* parishioners, not from the community at large. As long as he can hold and reasonably build his particular church, he has little to worry about.

In addition, if some members of the particular church begin to doubt the minister, for any reason, they either leave and join another church, or fight to get rid of him. If they succeed in the latter effort, then the struggle is over. The pastor leaves and the break is clean, usually with the pro-pastor faction following the minister out of the church. In any case, the internal church struggle is very seldom a long, drawn-out battle, lasting, that is, for years. In interviews, several ministers confirmed this observation. One stated: "Sure, you get church splits and so forth all the time. And believe me, they can be nasty. But they don't last. It's not something that just simmers and simmers." Another minister who was involved in such a battle a few years ago stated:

> I saw it coming. This little group just kept agitating and agitating. First one thing and then another. So I just called a church meeting one night and we just had it out. Took a vote and the Lord voted with our side. And I just told them, I said: "That settles it. I'm staying and we're going to stop all this foolish nonsense." Some left and joined another church. But that was it, and the rest of us were glad to see 'em go. Good riddance. Lord knows. I tell you.

There is the important factor of pride parishioners have in their church. Members of a church do not like to be associated with a church which has a reputation of constant internal disputes and turmoil. One deacon stated:

> It's embarrassing, you know. You say you belong to such and such a church, and folks right away know that

that's the place where they're always fighting the pastor, and they don't join. And folks start to talking about how God's not in that church and so forth and so on. It's embarrassing. So you try to keep away from a mess like that.

The norm, then, is for internal harmony to prevail most of the time. Where there are intrachurch battles, they come and go rather quickly, with usually a very clear resolution of the problem.

For many black people, the church is the only institution they belong to which is decidedly and exclusively theirs. It is important, therefore, that they protect it and be completely comfortable with it and in it. They must have complete confidence in the competence and integrity of the minister. The church service for many participants is one moment in their lives when they can be open, free, relaxed, themselves.

Du Bois, at the turn of the century, described the function of deception in the lives of the weak and subordinated. It has been necessary to lie at times in order to survive:

> To-day the young Negro of the South who would succeed cannot be frank and outspoken, honest and self-assertive, but rather he is daily tempted to be silent and wary, politic and shy; he must flatter and be pleasant, endure petty insults with a smile, shut his eyes to wrong; in too many cases he sees positive personal advantage in deception and lying. His real thoughts, his real aspirations, must be guarded in whispers; he must not criticise, he must not complain.[7]

The church service permitted them the opportunity to shout if they felt so moved and to let their full emotions show. During slavery and even afterwards in some areas of the South, however, it was still necessary at times for the preacher to couch his sermons in cryptic terms, lest the white boss-overseer punish him. Some spirituals had a double meaning—the Promised Land was both heaven and the North. But even with these constraints, the church-goers could maximize their chance to let go, to sing and shout and to approach a condition of comfort not ever permitted in the everyday struggle for sheer economic survival.

Indeed, it was apparently this sort of situation that caused one ex-slave to state how he felt about black preachers on the plantation:

> Old Master was a fine Christian but he like his juleps anyways. He let us niggers have preachings and prayers and would give us a parole to go ten or fifteen miles to a camp meeting and stay two or three days with nobody but Uncle John to stand for us. *Mostly we had white preachers, but when we had a black preacher that was heaven.*[8]

Many black worshipers, then and now, identify with the preacher because of his ability to fill these very important needs. He creates an atmosphere, putting his people in touch with God, in which pressures are at least momentarily lifted. Henry H. Mitchell describes it in the following way:

> In a world of forced, hurried conformity, the Black Church remains an oasis where God and his children meet and talk to each other. "Freedom" is the key word describing this experience. Man is free. God is free. Nobody is under pressure.[9]

When there is tension and turmoil within the church, this freedom is not possible to experience. Without question, there is competition between church clubs—the Willing Workers' Club vies with the Busy Bee Club to raise more money for the new Sunday-school building—but this is friendly, permissible competition, all geared toward doing "the Lord's work." But factional fighting with the minister or between various groups is frowned upon severely. Therefore considerable effort is expended by the preacher and the parishioners to minimize those situations which make relaxed, comfortable worship difficult or impossible. Conflict is eschewed; consensus becomes a very high priority, and one will find exceptional efforts made to suppress potentially divisive situations.

One member of a deacon board described how his board went to great lengths to protect their preacher from public exposure when it was discovered that the minister was having an adulterous affair with a lady in the choir. Those efforts included giving alibis for the minister's occasional absences from week-night meetings. And only after several months was the board finally able to get rid of the minister. "We just didn't give him a raise when he asked for one. We said the budget couldn't afford it. He knew then that we didn't appreciate his shenanigans, and he'd better make other plans. He was a good enough preacher, and people kept joining, but his carryings-on would hurt the church sooner or later, and we couldn't stand for that."

Notwithstanding, the deacon indicated that the few church officials who knew about the affair did not speak to the parties involved, because "we just didn't want the word to get out more than it was. We knew something had to be done about it, though." It was clear that the entire episode was very painful to the deacon. He was ashamed of his pastor, the choir member, his own role, and he was quite relieved to have it finished.

There is another aspect of the relationship of the black preacher to his people that must be noted. It is not uncommon in some circles to hear black people compare white and black professionals so that the latter come off unfavorably. This is, in part, a function of the attitude

that white professionals—especially doctors, dentists, lawyers—have a better training, and it may also be a result of
the feeling that white lawyers, for example, have more
influence "downtown," that a white lawyer "can get to the
judge." Occasionally one hears a black patient berate a
black doctor as being not qualified or as being interested
only in money. Or a black client will state that a black
lawyer does not know as much law as the average white
lawyer, and thus the client prefers a white doctor or lawyer. In the reverse, a black doctor will complain that his
black patients are lax in paying their bills. This is referred
to as the "opposite-number syndrome." *

Benjamin Mays remarked about this phenomenon when
he wrote:

> Much progress has been made in this area since 1926,
> but many Negroes still have a long way to go before
> they can rid themselves of the false notion that a white
> professional is necessarily better qualified than a black
> one. I once heard Bishop Hickman of the AME Church
> tell this story: A Negro woman, talking to her next-
> door neighbor, Mrs. B., told her that their mutual
> friend, Mrs. C., was ill. "How sick is she?" queried
> Mrs. B. "She's sick enough to have a white doctor!"
> was the reply. Systematic undermining of self-confi-
> dence has done damaging things to black people.[10]

Such an attitude does not persist about black preachers.
In fact, what one finds frequently is just the reverse. As
the ex-slave said: When a black preacher is in the pulpit,
that's heaven! Black parishioners generally feel that their
black preacher is far superior to any white preacher. Invariably, blacks prefer their black preacher to white
preachers, and this preference dates back to earliest times.

* This phrase was suggested to me by a young black graduate student,
Mr. Raymond Richardson.

Black preachers, it is felt, have greater oratorical skills; they have a greater awareness of the intimate problems affecting black lives, and they are able to speak to those problems.[11] In addition, the black preacher can refer to their common background and experiences and receive volumes of sympathetic responses from his listeners, who feel the preacher to be one of them.

Thus, over the years a very personal relationship has developed between the black preacher and his parishioners. This has been demonstrated in the protective care some black church members show for their minister, buying him clothes, cars, food, sending him on European trips and generally seeing after his and his family's every personal need. And frequently this care is provided by church members who are themselves receiving welfare or barely eking out a living for their own families. An extraordinary and dramatic illustration of the devotion some blacks have for their minister is the act of two free black men during slavery days who voluntarily bound themselves in slavery while a slave preacher was freed for six months to raise money to purchase his freedom. The two voluntary slaves felt so strongly that the preacher was of value as a man of God and as a leader that they were willing to endure that servitude.[12] The minister successfully raised the money, and he subsequently established the First African Baptist Church of Philadelphia in 1809.

There has developed over several centuries a very close, almost familial tie between the black preacher and his people. They have come to rely heavily on each other, and they have come to know the strengths and weaknesses of each other. If a particular minister is not inclined toward civic action, there is no evidence that the membership will push or pressure him in that direction. More frequently, the case is just the opposite. It is the minister who usually has to push or cajole his parishioners to act on civic matters. Even then, however, he seldom goes too far. The evidence is that where there is a socially concerned minister, either the parishioners follow his lead or they remain silent or inactive, or they occasionally subtly hint that the minister should spend more time on "church business."

When the minister is not civically active, or when he even takes a public stand against such action, no great internal church disturbance develops over his inaction or his attitude. This is the case even though there may be various prominent members of the church who are quite active. One normally hears the rationalization that "At least he sure is a good preacher," or "He really takes care of the church and the members. He's there when you need him." This indicates the extent to which the strong ethos of attentiveness to strictly religious matters still prevails in many black churches. In other words, a preacher who did not want to involve himself in civic matters, especially racial matters of a civil-rights nature, would not be running the risk of incurring the ill-will of his members. (It is quite true that the opposite might be the case for those social-activist ministers, as we shall see in Chapter VII.)

Nor do the parishioners become involved in political debates between their pastor and another minister. The most notable instance of this is the case of Olivet Baptist Church on Chicago's South Side, one of the largest in the country with several thousand members. The pastor is Reverend Joseph H. Jackson, president of the National Baptist Convention, U.S.A., Inc., since 1953. Reverend Jackson has a reputation of being conservative on race issues, and beginning in the early 1960's, he publicly disagreed with the protest tactics of Martin Luther King, Jr., on more than one occasion. (It is important to note that in 1956, Reverend Jackson was very instrumental in raising money in his church to purchase two station wagons to be used by the Montgomery Improvement Association during the Montgomery bus boycott. Some people suggest that Jackson's disaffection with King began when the latter became associated with a faction seeking to replace Jackson as head of the Baptist Convention.) As popular as King was with many members of Olivet, there was never an issue made of Reverend Jackson's position. Some members supported King in the mass marches held for open housing in Chicago in the summer of 1966. Jackson condemned these marches. But the members continued to attend Olivet on Sunday. One member, a gentleman over forty years of age, stated, "Well, I'll tell you, I feel this way. It takes all kinds. My pastor serves the Lord his way, and Dr. King, before he was killed, served God in his. And I think both men have a point."

The disagreement between the two very powerful preachers, while extremely intense, did not affect the internal operation of the church. Even after Martin Luther King's death, when national sentiment was extremely favorable toward his memory, Reverend Jackson indicated his strong displeasure with King's actions. The Chicago City Council voted to change the name of South Park Boulevard to Dr. Martin Luther King, Jr., Drive. Olivet Baptist Church is on the corner of 31st and South Park Boulevard. Its original address was 3101 South Park Boulevard. When the street name was changed, Reverend Jackson had the address of the church changed to 401 East 31st Street!

It may well be, of course, that a less powerful minister than Reverend Jackson would not have been able to survive such action. Yet it is clear that he has survived without any *open* debates or pressure from his members to change his views or his actions. He is considered one of the best, as well as most influential and powerful, preachers in the country, and this is apparently more than sufficient for his parishioners. One member of Olivet stated: "We come to hear the word of God, and that man can tell it to you. That's the point."

"Son, if they ain't talking loud, they ain't preaching"

The black culture is characterized by an oral tradition. Knowledge, attitudes, ideas, notions are traditionally transmitted orally, not through the written word. It is not unusual, then, that the natural leader among black people would be one with exceptional oratorical skills. He must be able to talk, to speak—to preach. In the black religious tradition, the successful black preacher *is* an expert orator. His role involves more, however. His relationship with his parishioners is reciprocal; he talks to them, and they *talk back* to him. This is expected. In many church circles, this talk-back during a sermon is a firm measure of the preacher's effectiveness. The congregation becomes involved.

Thus, many preachers have developed the speaking habit of eliciting responses with such injections as "Have I got a witness?" or "You ought to say a-men!" The popular, young Reverend Jesse Jackson (he refers to himself as "just a country preacher") of Operation PUSH (People United to Save Humanity) frequently intersperses his sermon-speeches with "Y'all know what I'm talking 'bout?"

The congregation responds with a variety of expressions: "Go 'head on." "Well, all right!" "Yes, yes." "Help him, Lord!" "Preach the word." "Come on."

During the spring of 1968, SCLC (Southern Christian Leadership Conference) conducted the Poor People's Campaign in Washington. For several weeks thousands of people, mostly black and poor, camped on public grounds in the nation's capital. The overall purpose was to pressure the federal government into enacting meaningful legislation to aid poor people in this country. Resurrection City, as the campsite came to be called, was inundated for weeks with rain and mud. Internal friction, conflict and fights among groups were almost a daily occurrence. And it is accurate to say that the campaign did not achieve the primary purpose it set out to achieve. But when spirits were low—which became increasingly the case as the days and weeks passed—mass meetings were held which were addressed by preachers with great oratorical skills for reaching and revitalizing sagging spirits. Charles Fager has captured one such event:

> Friday night a Campaign mass meeting was held at St. Stephen's Baptist Church, where the church was full and the crowd unusually boisterous. The featured preacher of the evening was Rev. C. L. Franklin of Detroit. Rev. Franklin is the father of Miss Aretha Franklin, a very successful soul singer, and he was an old friend of Dr. King. A solidly built man with sleek shiny hair and a booming voice, Rev. Franklin was a real master of the black Baptist preacher's art; he enjoyed his work, and the crowd enjoyed him. His sermon was free-form development of the theme, "They Wouldn't Bow," from the Bible account of Shadrach, Meshach and Abednego, who were placed in a fiery furnace for their refusal to worship the pagan gods of Babylon.
>
> "I hope I can get somebody to pray with me tonight," he began, warming them up, "because you know, I'm a *Negro* preacher, and I like to talk to people and have people talk *back* to me." He paused while they roared their pleasure. "I want to talk to you tonight about 'They Wouldn't Bow.'" [13]

The Reverend C. L. Franklin proceeded to preach, eliciting a full response from the audience at the end of virtually every five or six words he spoke. Charles Fager continues:

Franklin's delivery crossed the line between speaking and singing as he rose toward a crescendo, and the responses from the crowd became tumultuous and almost continuous, beyond hope of reproduction in print. The roots of his famous daughter's vocal style could be heard reverberating in his voice. At the climax he suddenly turned and sat down, leaving the crowd in mid-cheer. But it was only a flourish; he was on his feet again in a few seconds, shouting and singing to them and with them, finally leading the church in the hymn, "I'm Gonna Trust in the Lord Until I Die," and then sitting down exhausted, dramatically wiping his streaming face with a large white handkerchief.

It was a magnificent performance, unequalled during the Campaign in brilliance of delivery or frenzy of response. It was the closest the Washington mass meetings ever came to the kind of exultation that makes a movement the center of a community's attention the way it was in Selma.[14]

Some observers might interpret this kind of verbal interaction as mere emotionalism. Henry H. Mitchell sees it rooted in the black African culture:

The Black style, which includes the pattern of call-and-response, is very easily traceable to Black African culture. Such response requires a participating audience. Black preaching has had an audience from the beginning. It has been shaped by interaction with that audience—hammered out in dialogue with the Black Brothers and Sisters. If the Black preaching tradition is unique, then that uniqueness depends in part upon the uniqueness of the Black congregation which talks back to the preacher as a normal part of the pattern of worship.[15]

Such behavior is mostly associated with the Baptist and the Pentecostal churches and with what are commonly called the "sanctified" churches. It is found less in the

Methodist churches, and it is virtually nonexistent in the Presbyterian, Episcopalian and other denominations generally associated with middle- or upper-class status. Thus this behavior is seen essentially as lower-class behavior. But one Baptist minister, who stated that he encouraged shouting and talk-back, had another explanation:

> Son, those colored folks in those other churches, they're in white folks' churches. Anytime you find our people belonging to a church where you ain't suppose to open your mouth and tell the Lord just how good you feel, then you know that ain't a church for our folks. Of course, we shout and they talk to me—they helping me when they do that, 'cause you see we worshiping the Lord *together*. And I'll tell you, wherever you see one of *our* churches, and if the Lord's in that church, then you better believe, you gonna hear some noise.

This is another area in which a preacher and his people soon find out about each other and develop a harmonious relationship or a quick parting of ways. If a minister is not generally disposed to deliver the kind of sermon that elicits interaction, and if his congregation disagrees and wants such an atmosphere, the minister will not stay at that church very long. He may have a few Sundays now and then when "the spirit just didn't reach me," but these cannot be too often. "First," one minister stated, "you start to notice that the collection plates get lighter, then the attendance falls off. Then there's trouble."

The preacher and his people are more often than not in thorough agreement on the style and substance of the service they want. If the preacher simply cannot deliver, he moves on, and the "call" is sent out for another. And one of the first things a minister knows about a congregation is that it either is or is not "a shouting church." If *it* is, and *he* doesn't, *he* stays *away*. Seldom does one find a situation in which either the minister or the congregation tries to persuade or convert the other to a different style or tempo.

A Linkage Figure

One of the most crucial facts about black people in the United States is that they have been subjected to three dynamic and, at times, traumatic experiences involving abrupt cultural transformations. Each of these occurrences has had serious implications for the disruption of social institutions of the race and for the ways in which black people have attempted to meet and adapt to these abrupt changes in their lives.

The first occurred with their capture and sale into slavery and their transportation thousands of miles to a new land, language and fundamentally different way of life. This move, of course, was aggravated by the traumatic experience of the Middle Passage, during which, records indicate, they were packed under inhuman conditions on cargo ships, and many, instead of submitting to the barbarities of their new condition, threw themselves overboard and chose death over permanent human debilitation. Lerone Bennett, Jr., has written:

> They were packed like books on shelves into holds which in some instances were no higher than eighteen inches. . . . Here, for the six to ten weeks of the voyage, the slaves lived like animals. Under the best conditions, the trip was intolerable. When epidemics of dysentery or smallpox swept the ships, the trip was beyond endurance.[16]

Such conditions could only be traumatic and they required a human being's full measure of strength to survive.

The second major experience was the change from slavery to freedom. After approximately 250 years of bondage, a legal condition was changed. The former slaves were not given "forty acres and a mule," and they were not given sufficient support in the art of surviving in their new, unprotected condition. They were, consequently, free to be further exploited and devastated. This, again, was an abrupt cultural transformation into a society no less hostile than it was under conditions of legal servitude. The adaptive social institutions they had been able to build up during time on the slave plantation were, for the most part, obliterated, and many freedmen simply wandered and drifted, trying to reunite families torn apart by a war and slavery. They were free in theory only. But politically, economically and educationally, they were still the dregs of society. Black Codes were passed by many states which circumscribed the lives of black people; and blacks had to start the protracted process of trying to pull themselves up by their bootstraps when they had no boots to wear, and few available means to acquire any. They were pawns in the political process of the larger society. When it suited the powers of the Republican North to use them against the Southern Confederacy, they did so during Reconstruction, beginning in 1867. When Northern industry no longer felt it in its interests to impose harsh penalties on the defeated Southern agriculturalists, the blacks were left stranded at the mercies of their former slaveholders, beginning with the Hayes-Tilden Compromise of 1876, which ended Reconstruction and effectively turned Southern state governments back to former slaveholders. Thus, the several decades following Emancipation were a period of abrupt cultural transformation.

The third such experience was the mass movement of black people out of the South to the North, beginning during World War I, accelerating during the interwar period and reaching its peak during and after World War II. The blacks left an agrarian, personal, informal, slower-paced environment and came into an industrial, impersonal, formal, faster-paced society. The elevated trains in Chicago and the subways of New York were nowhere in the culture of rural Mississippi and South Carolina; and it took profound adjustment to negotiate this new environment. Credit at the general store in rural Georgia was not something one filled out long application forms for and then waited to hear by mail about whether one "had got some credit." In the South, people could do much of their living out of doors and for much longer periods during the year—vegetable gardens could be planted at the door steps, fishing was possible in a nearby creek.

In all three instances, the black people have had their social institutions disrupted, either deliberately or through force of circumstances. In the transition from Africa to America, the extended-family tribal units were obliterated and deliberate policies pursued to break up families. Rituals from native, indigenous cultures were forbidden, and slaves from the same tribe at times were explicitly separated to guard against potential revolts and escape attempts. After Emancipation, the freedmen were left on their own, in most cases without property or legal protection of any kind and at the economic mercy of whites waiting to take advantage of them. A culture of enforced dependency maintained during slavery was now transformed into a culture of superficial independency. In the mass migrations northward, crowded ghettos awaited them, and they were required to adjust to an urban, concrete-sidewalk environment totally different from the rural, agrarian South they had known for centuries.

The one institution and the one individual the blacks had to rely on in bridging these transitional periods were the church and the preacher. The preacher became, then, a linkage figure, having to link up the old with the new, the familiar with the unfamiliar, tradition with modernity. In many cases, the black church was an adaptive institution. It was not wholly African, and it by no means was entirely Anglican or Western. Improvisation was required, and the black preacher was the master improviser.

Because of his role as leader and spokesman, he had frequent contacts with whites and the larger society, and he could interpret those forces to his people and teach crucial technique: How to survive on the plantation; how to "get next to" or "on the good side of" the plantation boss. Where to get a job in a segregated, discriminating, rural South; how to escape a potential lynch mob. How to apply for welfare (known as "relief" in the 1930's and 1940's) in the Northern cities when people were laid off from their low-paying jobs; where to find another kitchenette apartment when the absentee landlord in the old one "wouldn't do right" in making repairs.

He knew his people, and he came to know the many new obstacles and forces with which they had to cope in order to survive—not to mention thrive.

His role was the one familiar role carried over from the previous situation. And a bewildered, beleaguered people could identify with it even though it had to be played out under drastically different circumstances. Probably the only similarity between a small backwoods church in Alabama surrounded by forests and footpaths and a storefront church in Harlem surrounded by tenements and taverns was the man—the preacher—who stood up front in the pulpit. He was "God's man"—on that slave plantation, in that dirt-road Southern town, on the sidewalks of Detroit —and he was there to comfort them and to tell them, as he always had, that "the Lord will make a way, if you just believe in Him and be born again."

The black preacher linked up things. And for a people

who had had their lives and their cultures shattered, fragmented and torn asunder so often and so abruptly, this
linkage figure was important. (This is not to say that every
black preacher plays this role by consciously and overtly
relating his sermons to matters of this world. Many preachers seldom discuss social problems directly, and obviously
many preachers are not very knowledgeable about things
such as bureaucratic red tape in big cities. Those who are
ignorant of such matters can offer little help to their parishioners.) By their mere presence and continued leadership, the black preachers offer a steady figure with which
the people can identify. They represent continuity and, in
an important sense, stability—the only stable strand in the
lives of many people who have been wracked by instability
and abrupt changes.

II

The Ministry During Slavery

In many ways, one could make the argument that black people needed their preachers more during slavery than at any other time in their history in this country. This would be a tenable position in view of the obvious fact that the slaves had so few, if any, alternative outlets for self-expression and socializing other than religion. Religious practices allowed by the slave owners varied from place to place and from time to time, but at no time did one find religious services sanctioned which were calculated to lead to emancipation of the slaves. Thus, where the black preacher was permitted to serve the slaves, he was expected by the slaveholders to pacify the slaves and to reconcile them to their lowly lot here on earth.

Some preachers performed that function well, and they were rewarded by the whites for it.

In other instances, the black preachers provided a kind of solace for their people. While they might have preached pacification, they also gave aid and comfort and provided emotional inspiration. This could be seen, in a sense, as a survival mechanism.

It is also clear that some black preachers, especially in the North, but in a few isolated places in Southern slave states as well, vehemently opposed slavery and exhorted their people to rise up against the system by force and violence, if necessary.

Therefore, there is no one stance that black preachers took during this prolonged period of slavery. But there is overwhelming evidence that the slaves preferred their own black preachers to white preachers. The church meetings were fun, and the black preaching frequently was masterful. One ex-slave in Mississippi described her experiences in the following manner:

> De most fun we had was at our meetin's. We had dem most every Sunday and dey lasted way into de night. De preacher I liked de best was named Matthew Ewing. He was a comely nigger, black as night, and he sure could read out of his hand. He never learned no real readin' and writin' but he sure knowed his Bible and would hold his hand out and make like he was readin' and preach de purtiest preachin' you ever heard. De meetin's last from early in de mornin' till late at night. When dark come, de men folks would hang up a wash pot, bottom upwards, in de little brush church house us had, so's it would catch de noise and de overseer wouldn't hear us singin' and shoutin'. Dey didn't mind us meetin' in de daytime, but dey thought iffen we stayed up half de night we wouldn't work so hard de next day—and dat was de truth.
>
> You shoulda seen some of de niggers get religion. De best way was to carry 'em to de cemetery and let'em stand over a grave. Dey would start singin' and shoutin' about seein' fire and brimstone. Den dey would sing some more and look plumb sanctified.[2]

Frequently, the slave owners had white preachers preach to the slaves, and their sermons were constant admonitions to obey the masters: " 'Serve your masters. Don't steal your master's turkey. Don't steal your master's chickens. Don't

steal your master's hogs. Don't steal your master's meat.
Do whatsomeever your master tell you to do.' Same old
thing all de time." [3] There were no sermons from white
preachers on the plantations reminding the slaves of future
rewards in heaven. The reference to rewards in heaven
would imply that life on this earth was somehow unjusti-
fied in terms of hardships for slaves. Such a notion could
plant the seed for thinking that slavery was unjust and
that there should be resistance against it. "Dey did allow
us to go to church on Sunday about two miles down de
public road, and dey hired a white preacher to us. He
never did tell us nothing but 'Be good servants, pick up
old marse and old misses' things about de place, don't steal
no chickens or pigs, and don't lie about nothing.' Den dey
baptize you and call dat you got religion. Never did say
nothing about a slave dying and going to Heaven." [4]

At times a black preacher would be hired to preach to
the slaves, and to tell them that they had to obey if they
wanted to go to heaven. But when not supervised, the
black preacher would deviate from his orders. "A yellow
man [5] preached to us. She [the slave owner] had him preach
how we was to obey our master and missy if we want to go
to heaven, but when she wasn't there, he come out with
straight preachin' from the Bible." [6] Thus many slaves
knew the difference between the imposed, enforced slave
religion and "true Bible religion." And many of them
looked to their black preachers to provide the latter. They
could trust the black preacher to preach the "true word of
God," while at the same time they could see the contradictions and hypocrisy in the teachings and preachings of the
white, slave owner's imposed religion. One ex-slave re-
corded his reactions to this:

> Dey would take a great string of slaves in de road on
> Sunday and make us walk to church. Buggies with de
> white folks in would be in front of us, in de midst of

us, and all betwixt and behind us. When we got dat
four or five miles we had to sit on a log in de broiling
sun, while a white man preached to us. All dey ever
would say would be: "Niggers, obey your masters and
mistress and don't steal from 'em." And, lo and behold,
de masters would make us slaves steal from each of the
slave owners. Our master would make us surround a
herd of his neighbor's cattle, round dem up at night,
and make us slaves stay up all night long and kill and
skin every one of dem critters, salt the skins down in
layers in de master's cellar, and put de cattle piled
ceilin' high in de smokehouse so nobody could identify
skinned cattle.

Den when de sheriff would come around lookin' for
all dem stolen critters, our boss would say, "Sheriff,
just go right on down to dem niggers' cabins and search
dem good. I know my niggers don't steal." 'Course de
sheriff come to our cabins and search. Sure we didn't
have nothin' didn't belong to us, but de boss had
plenty. After de sheriff's search, we had to salt and
smoke all dat stolen meat and hang it in Old Marse's
smokehouse for him. Den dey tell us, don't steal.[7]

The authority, credibility and integrity of the slave
owner and the white preacher were undermined, if not
openly questioned. And when the black preacher was a
party to this kind of hypocrisy, he was seen as no more
than a tool used by the owners in the same way the slaves
were used. Many slaves understood his plight, precisely
because it was basically little different from theirs. He had
to play a game and submit to constraints imposed upon
him in much the same manner as the other slaves.

In the North prior to Emancipation, some black preachers who were members of white denominations also had
constraints imposed on them by whites. Peter Williams, Jr.,
the first black ordained as a priest in the Episcopal Church,
served as rector of the black congregation, St. Philip's

Church, in New York City from 1818 until 1849. His father
was one of the founders of the independent African Methodist Episcopal Zion Church. But the son remained within
the white denomination. During this period, there was
intense concern over the issues of colonization of blacks
and abolition of slavery. At first Reverend Peter Williams,
Jr., took an active part in these debates, but then the bishops of the Episcopal Church decided that he should be
silenced and they ordered him to confine his ministry to
the Gospel and to stay out of political affairs. He acqui-
esced. The Episcopal Church did not want to take a stand
on the issues and risk embarrassment. These kinds of sanctions were not possible, of course, where black people
organized their own independent churches. The black
historian Carter G. Woodson offered a rationale for Peter
Williams' acquiescence:

> It does not appear that he had that moral stamina
> to impel him to renounce his connection with a church
> seeking to muzzle a man praying for the deliverance of
> his people. It may be, however, that since he was too
> far advanced in years to make any radical change in
> his course, he followed the orders of his superiors.[8]

Williams resigned from the Board of Managers of the
New York Anti-Slavery Society, and his statement was
printed in the Society's newspaper, *African Repository,* on
July 14, 1834:

> My Bishop, without giving his opinions on the sub-
> ject of Abolition, has now advised me, in order that the
> Church under my care "may be found on the Christian
> side of meekness, order, and self-sacrifice to the com-
> munity," to resign connection with the Anti-Slavery
> Society, and to make public my resignation. . . . By
> the transaction of last Friday evening, my Church is
> now closed, and I have been compelled to leave my

people. Whether I shall be permitted to return to them again, I cannot say, but whether or not, I have the satisfaction of feeling that I have laboured earnestly and sincerely for their temporal and spiritual benefit, and the promotion of the public good. . . . Having given this simple and faithful statement of facts; I now, in conformity to the advice of my Bishop, publicly resign my station as a member of the Board of Managers of the Anti-Slavery Society, and of its executive committee, without, however, passing my opinion respecting the principles on which that society is founded.

(This matter of freedom to take stands was no small factor in motivating some blacks to establish their own independent churches. Reverend Kelly Goodwin of Winston-Salem, North Carolina, discusses the freedom of black preachers compared to that of white preachers in Chapter VII.)

It was not uncommon during slavery to find black preachers serving white congregations, in the South as well as in the North. A black soldier during the Revolutionary War, Lemuel Haynes, served as pastor of white churches in Connecticut, Vermont and New York from the 1780's to his death in 1833. Married to a white woman in 1783, he was a minister in the Congregational Church, and during his pastorates he took an active part in political affairs.

Samuel Ringgold Ward served as an outspoken black minister of white Presbyterian churches in New York State. He strongly advocated abolition of slavery, frequently spending more time and effort on political freedom and rights of blacks than on preaching the gospel.

Even in the South, black preachers at times spoke to and pastored all-white congregations. This was the case with a slave preacher named Caesar, whose freedom the (white) Alabama Baptist Association purchased in 1828 for $625 to have him preach among whites as well as blacks.

Another slave preacher, George Bentley, in Tennessee

refused to have his freedom purchased by his congregation
—which consisted of whites and blacks—because he did not
wish to leave his master.

It is clear that these black preachers in the South during
slavery who ministered to whites and blacks were not flam-
ing abolitionists like some of their counterparts in the
North. The Southern preachers, instead, were noted for
their great oratorical skills, their literal knowledge of the
Scriptures and their devotion to the maintenance of the
status quo. Many were loyal to their masters, and this loyalty was rewarded by allowing them as much time as they
needed to tend to their ministerial duties.

The fact remains, however, that the black preacher in
those instances where he served as pastor for whites was
the only person of his race during slavery who occupied a
position of authority before whites. He spoke; whites listened. This reversal of roles surely must have been important and impressive to blacks, and it must to a certain
extent have added to the prestige, if not the power, of the
black preacher. This would be the case regardless of the
content of his message. This is speculative, obviously; there
is no historical evidence to support this judgment. But it is
reasonable to imagine that some slaves would be impressed
by a black man who stood before whites and spoke authoritatively on a subject of apparent interest and concern to
whites.

Emphasis on the Next World

It is impossible to calculate how many black preachers
during and in slavery preached sermons calling on their
fellow slaves to endure their present hardships, and how
many advocated the overthrow of the system. One could
assume, however, that if the master permitted the preacher
to hold religious services on the plantation, the emphasis

was on the former theme, not the latter. In some instances, the master saw the role of the black preacher as a pacifier, and some preachers played that role. They admonished the slaves to be obedient, loyal to their masters and to endure the pains and problems of this life and to look forward to better things to come in the life hereafter. The Reverend Israel Campbell was so good in this regard that several slave owners sought to buy him in order for him to preach continually to their slaves.

The Reverend Jupiter Hammon was another slave preacher who delivered a message pleasing to the masters:

> There are some things very encouraging in God's word, for such ignorant creatures as we are; for God hath not chosen the rich of this world. Not many rich, not many noble are called, but God hath chosen the weak things of this world, and things which are not, to confound the things that are: And when the great and the rich refused coming to the gospel feast, the servant was told to go into the highways, and hedges, and compel those poor creatures that he found there, to come in. Now my bretheren, it seems to me, that there are no people that ought to attend to the hope of happiness in another world so much as we. Most of us are cut off from comfort and happiness here in this world, and can expect nothing from it. Now seeing this is the case, why should we not take care to be happy after death. Why should we spend our whole lives in sinning against God: And be miserable in this world and in the world to come.[9]

But some slaves were less interested in a message of obedience to the slave master than in a sermon calling for obedience to the Lord. In such instances, it was clear that there was—in the minds of some slaves—a distinct difference between the two. Obedience to God might not have meant revolt and abolition of slavery, but a sermon calling for obedience to the slave master was not what some slaves understood to be religion. A religious service was seen as a comfort, a place to momentarily relieve one's burdens, and if it did not provide this, it was not successful. A slave preacher could emphasize the comforts of the next world, but he was seen as no different from a white preacher if all he preached was obedience to the master. And while the slave understood the constraints on the black preacher, he nonetheless did not relish that kind of sermon to relieve his misery. One ex-slave made the following observation:

> Sometimes the master sent me alone to the grinding mill. Load in the yellow corn, hitch in the oxen, I was ready to go. I gets me fixed up with a pass and takes to the road. That was the trip I like best. On the way was a still. Off in the brush. If the still was lonely I stop, not on the way but on the way back. Mighty good whiskey, too! Maybe I drinks too much, then I was sorry. Not that I swipe the whiskey, just sorry because I gets sick!
>
> Then I figures a woods camp meeting will steady me up and I goes. The preacher meet me and want to know how is my feelings. I says I is low with the misery and he say to join up with the Lord. I never join because he don't talk about the Lord. Just about the master and mistress. How the slaves must obey around the plantation—how the white folks know what is good for the slaves. Nothing about obeying the Lord and working for him. I reckon the old preacher was worrying more about the bullwhip than he was the Bible, else he say something about the Lord! But I always obeys the Lord—that's why I is still living! [10]

Many spirituals sung in the churches emphasized what Benjamin Mays called the "compensatory" idea, that God will reward pain and suffering in the next life, in heaven.

> The creation of the Spirituals was hardly an accident in Negro life. It was a creation born of necessity in order that the slave might more adequately adjust him-

self to the new conditions in the new world. . . . God saves for Heaven those who hold out to the end. He provides golden crowns, slippers, robes, and eternal life for the righteous. The principal reward comes in the other world.[11]

And Mays concluded that the ideas in the early sermons of the black preachers were very similar to the ideas found in the spirituals.

Thus comfort and pacification were two main functions of the preacher. A strong criticism of religion in black history has been that it has served as an opiate, that it taught blacks to be meek, humble and kind, to turn the other cheek. Clearly, this has been one result—not exclusively, of course, as will be shown in the following section —as illustrated by the statement of one ex-slave:

One old lady named Emily Moorehead runned in and held my mother once for Phipps to whip her. And my mother was down with consumption too. I aimed to get old Phipps for that. But then I got religion and I couldn't do it. Religion makes you forget a heap of things.[12]

Forgetting "a heap of things," particularly any ideas connected with fighting back and attempting to revolt against slavery, was precisely what the slave owners wanted. And any black preacher who could perform that function was a valuable asset to the masters. George Liele was such a preacher. He was born in Virginia before the Revolutionary War, and was so effective as a preacher who pacified fellow slaves that his master freed him to permit him to devote himself full-time to his ministerial duties. He would not preach or minister to any slaves who had not received prior permission from their owners.[13]

His influence among the masters and overseers became unusual, and the membership of his church increased rapidly. No literature was used and no instruction given until it had at first been shown to the members of the legislature, the magistrates, and the justices to secure their permission beforehand. One of the masters speaking of the wholesome influence of Liele's preaching, said that he did not need to employ an assistant nor to make use of the whip whether he was at home or elsewhere, as his slaves were industrious and obedient, and lived together in unity, brotherly love and peace.[14]

"Uncle Jack" was a similar black preacher who lived and preached in Virginia for forty years after the Revolutionary War. He was considered so valuable by the whites that they bought his freedom and purchased a small farm for him in Virginia. He preached from plantation to plantation and, interestingly, he was able to convert many whites to the Baptist church.

There was another type of black preacher during slavery who neither taught violent resistance against slavery nor sanctioned slavery and racial discrimination. Richard Allen is the best example. It was Allen and two other blacks, Absalom Jones and William White, who were expelled from the white St. George's Church in Philadelphia in 1787.[15] This act led Allen to establish the Free African Society, which subsequently resulted in the founding of the African Methodist Episcopal Church in 1816, with Allen as the first black bishop. The irony is that Allen himself had preached many sermons from the pulpit of St. George's Church before the incident in 1787. The white congregation, however, had become increasingly disturbed by the growing number of blacks attending the church services.

Although the Free African Society under Allen's influence passed strong resolutions calling for the abolition of slavery, Allen could not be considered an advocate of freedom "by any means necessary." Many of his sermons counseled slaves to love and obey their masters, because in doing so, they (the slaves) would be rewarded in heaven. He urged his people "not to hold malice or ill-will" against the slave owners. But he also felt that slavery was against God's will, and slave owners would be punished by God if they did not free their slaves. Allen's message was the classic example of emphasis on the next world. In his address "To the People of Color," he said:

> I mention experience to you, that your hearts may not sink at the discouraging prospects you may have, and that you may put your trust in God, who sees your condition, and as a merciful father pitieth his children, so doth God pity them that love Him; and as your hearts are inclined to serve God, you will feel an affectionate regard towards your masters and mistresses, so called, and the whole family in which you live. This will be seen by them, and tend to promote your liberty, especially with such as have feeling masters; and if they are otherwise, you will have the favor and love of God dwelling in your hearts; which you will value more than anything else, which will be a consolation in the worst condition you can be in, and no master can deprive you of it; and as life is short and uncertain, and the chief end of our having a being in this world is to be prepared for a better, I wish you to think of this more than anything else; then you will have a view of that freedom which the sons of God enjoy; and if the trouble of your condition end with your lives, you will be admitted to the freedom which God hath prepared for those of all colors that love him. Here the power of the most cruel masters ends, and all sorrow and tears are wiped away.[16]

Allen abhorred slavery, but he felt its abolition should not come about as a result of attempts at violent overthrow by the slaves. He also rejected ideas of colonization for black people. He was part of a group of three thousand blacks who met in Philadelphia in 1817 and condemned the idea of colonization as an "outrage, having no other object in view than the benefit of the slaveholding interests of the country." [17]

Perhaps Allen had been influenced by his own experiences. Born a slave, he was able to purchase his freedom for two thousand dollars from a slave master who had become convinced that slavery was wrong—but who apparently felt obliged to receive compensation for expiating his wrongful act of holding slaves. It was precisely this kind of contradiction that weakened Allen's moral argument, whether he recognized it or not. There might well have been those "feeling masters" who would "promote your liberty," but for a price.

In many ways, the views of Allen coincide with those of latter-day black preachers involved in civil-rights action, especially in the 1960's. While they preside over all-black churches, a major reason for this is the traditional exclusion of blacks, as parishioners and as preachers, from white churches. Richard Allen was no more a black nationalist than Martin Luther King, Jr., but both men developed from a base of an all-black religious constituency. Both could be called "integrationists." Both were strong advocates of the power of love and forgiveness; and both made strong appeals to whites to act justly and to be merciful. Both eschewed violence, but they acted, in their respective ways, against racial injustice. In the case of Allen, it would be tempting to equate his founding of the A.M.E. Church with an act of "separatism," but that would not be an accurate understanding of the man. His motivation was to provide a more adequate base from which to enunciate his views, both religious and racial. The fact that he led the movement to establish an independent black church did not mean that he was not, throughout his career, a firm believer in the reconciliation of the races. He wanted a place where black Christians could worship in dignity, and that was the basic reason for pulling out of St. George's Church in 1787. In taking such a stand and leading the African Methodist Episcopal Church for several decades, he became, as historian Lerone Bennett, Jr., has noted, "the first national black leader," and president of the first black convention held in American history. The convention was held in Philadelphia in 1830 "to devise ways and means for the bettering of our condition." A second cenvention was called for the following year, but Richard Allen was unable to make it. He died on March 26, 1831, five months before another black preacher, Nat Turner, started on a different route to freedom for his people.

Several black bishops followed in the footsteps of Allen in the A.M.E. Church: Morris Brown, Daniel A. Payne, Edward Waters and William Paul Quinn. All of these men have had Southern black colleges named after them. Most of these men were self-educated. Their years of training were few but, like Daniel Alexander Payne, they were staunch advocates of learning and formal education. Payne was able to study only two years at Lutheran Theological Seminary in Gettysburg, and he was impatient with blacks who did not avail themselves of every opportunity to acquire as much education as possible. At times he referred to the "illiteracy of the itinerant ministry up to 1844" in the A.M.E. Church. He was born in South Carolina in 1811 and opened a school in Charleston in 1829. But in 1835, the South Carolina Legislature made effective a bill prohibiting anyone from teaching slaves how to read or write. (Any white person violating the law would be fined and imprisoned; a black person would be whipped and fined.) This law disturbed Payne intensely, and he indicated how he was tempted to question the existence of God as a result of the many hardships endured by the blacks. But again he overcame his doubting and renewed his faith:

> Sometimes it seemed as though some wild beast had plunged his fangs into my heart, and was squeezing out its life-blood. Then I began to question the existence of God, and to say: "If he does exist, is he just? If so, why does he suffer one race to oppress and enslave another, to rob them by unrighteous enactments of rights, which they hold most dear and sacred?" Sometimes I wished for the lawmakers what Nero wished— "that the Romans had but one neck." I would be the man to sever the head from its shoulders. Again said I: "Is there no God?" But then there came into my mind those solemn words. "With God one day is as a thousand years and a thousand years as one day. Trust in him, and he will bring slavery and all its outrages to an end." These words from the spirit world acted on my troubled soul like water on a burning fire, and my aching heart was soothed and relieved from its burden of woes.[18]

He chose to move North, where he "could teach without let or hindrance," firm in the belief that God had intended him to do that work. At one early stage in his ministerial career, he was offered three hundred dollars a year plus expenses to go on a lecture tour in behalf of the Anti-Slavery Society. He declined the offer for two reasons. He decided to travel with another minister to learn as much as he could, and he felt that his calling was as a preacher, not an abolitionist orator. He explained:

> There he endeavored to persuade me to travel with him, and among the inducements which he plied to my mind was the following statement: Said he, "Daniel, do you know what makes the master and servant? Nothing but superior knowledge—nothing but one man knowing more than another. Now, if you will go with

> me, the knowledge you may acquire will be of more
> value to you than three hundred dollars." . . . Imme-
> diately I seized the idea. Instead of going to travel as
> his servant, I went and chained my mind down to the
> study of science and philosophy, that I might obtain
> that knowledge which makes the master.[19]

And in giving his second reason, he indicated he felt that
his talents and destiny lay in other areas. Frederick Douglass was at that time a very famous black abolitionist who
spoke extensively in this country and abroad against slavery. Payne perceived that he was cut from different cloth,
and that God held the scissors:

> When God has a work to be executed he also chooses
> the man to execute it. He also qualifies the workman
> for the work. Frederick Douglass was fitted for his spe-
> cialty; Daniel Alexander Payne for his. Frederick Doug-
> lass could not do the work which was assigned to
> Daniel Alexander Payne, nor Daniel Alexander Payne
> the work assigned to Frederick Douglass. "The hour
> for the man, and the man for the hour." He who un-
> dertakes, through envy, jealousy, or any other motive
> or consideration, to reverse this divine law resists the
> purpose of the Almighty and brings misfortune, some-
> times ruin, upon himself.[20]

Many black preachers had a number of options—at least
more than their less fortunate brothers in slavery—open
to them, but they chose to pastor. The decisions frequently
were not easy, because then as now, for a people with so
many needs, there were so many functions to perform. And
this situation was aggravated when skills were in very short
supply.

As black preachers at times had to make career choices,
they also had to choose between competing organizational
structures. Nine years after Richard Allen left St. George's
Church in Philadelphia to form the A.M.E. Church, a

group of blacks in 1796 established the African Methodist Episcopal Zion Church in New York. Their break with the white Methodists was not as traumatic or simply dramatic as the schism in Philadelphia in 1787. But as Carter G. Woodson reports, they had a "desire for the privilege of holding meetings of their own, where they might have an opportunity to exercise their spiritual gifts among themselves, and thereby be more useful to one another." [21] After several years of internal struggling over whether to return to the white church, join Allen's A.M.E. Church, or remain independent as the A.M.E. Zion Church, they decided on the last and selected James Varick as their first bishop in 1822.

There have been a number of causes of schisms within the black church and among preachers, but one that receives less open attention in historical accounts is the factor of skin color. The matter of complexion of skin has been a major one throughout the history of black people in the United States. Obviously, this diversity of skin color stems essentially from the cohabitation of white men with slave women. Gunnar Myrdal observed:

> Many white fathers freed their illegitimate mulatto offspring and often also the children's mothers, or gave them the opportunity to work out their freedom on easy terms. Some were helped to education and sent to the free states in the North. Some were given a start in business or helped to acquire land.
>
> For this reason the free Negro population everywhere contained a greater proportion of mixed bloods than did the slave population. The mulattoes followed the white people's valuation and associated their privileges with their lighter color. They considered themselves superior to the black slave people and attributed their superiority to the fact of their mixed blood. The black slaves, too, came to hold this same valuation. The white

people, however, excluded even the fairest of the mulatto group from their own caste—in so far as they did
not succeed in passing—and the mulattoes, in their turn,
held themselves more and more aloof from the black
slaves and the humbler blacks among the free Negroes;
thus the mulattoes tended early to form a separate in-
termediary caste of their own. . . . Color thus became a badge of status and social distinction among the
Negro people.[22]

E. Franklin Frazier also notes the consequences of such
contacts between the slave and the master.

. . . in the United States it was generally the son of a
mulatto household servant who was apprenticed to
learn some skilled trade. The process of acculturation
was not restricted to learning the language of their
masters, certain work habits, and skill in the use of
tools. The close association between master and slave
on the plantation provided the means for the communication of ideas and beliefs, of morals and manners,
depending, of course, upon the type of social control.[23]

It could be expected that this problem would be felt
among the black ministry. An important observation, however, is that at particular historical times blacks have reacted to the phenomenon of skin color in different ways.

While there is validity to the overall generalization, the
lighter the complexion, the more favorably received by
even the blacks, occasionally blacks have deliberately attempted to project a dark-skinned person as their leader.
This seems to happen most usually in those cases in which
blacks are moving to organize, for any number of reasons,
along an all-black basis and are spending less effort on the
immediate goal of achieving integration. This was clearly
true of the Marcus Garvey movement in the 1920's which
was organized under the Universal Negro Improvement
Association. Garvey's highly nationalist movement empha-

sized blackness; he frequently questioned the racial commitment of some spokesmen, especially Du Bois, who were
of lighter complexion.

But in 1816, when the A.M.E. Church was being formed
in Philadelphia, the issue came up. The body first chose
Reverend Daniel Coker as the bishop; he declined the
next day, and Richard Allen was selected. Most accounts
of the incident state simply: ". . . but for several reasons
he resigned the next day in favor of Richard Allen"; [24] or
he ". . . declined election as the first bishop of the African Methodist Episcopal Church"; [25] or ". . . although he
declined the election." [26] Lerone Bennett, Jr., however,
added more to our knowledge of the circumstances when
he wrote:

> Allen, interestingly enough, was not chosen the first
> bishop. This honor went to Daniel Coker, an eloquent
> Baltimore preacher who was elected bishop on April
> 9, 1816, the first day of the conference. According to
> tradition, the light-skinned Coker, the son of a slave
> and a white woman, was too fair for some of the dele-
> gates. Coker was persuaded to resign and Richard Allen
> was elected bishop the next day.[27]

Thus, notwithstanding the facts that some men such as
Allen were not black nationalists in the strict sense of the
term and that there were undoubtedly delegates at the
conference who were not in agreement with the need to
have a darker-skinned man lead them, there were also
some delegates who thought otherwise. The impact of skin
color on the thinking of blacks is not as simplistic as some
accounts would make it seem. Then as now, there were
obviously tensions within the group over this issue, and
there were some, such as Allen, who recognized the cleav-
ages. Daniel A. Payne, who was five years old at the time
of that historic conference, later wrote of Richard Allen's

efforts to bring about such a reconciliation. His account intimates that Allen was not as innocent or as uninvolved in having Coker step aside as might at first be assumed. Most accounts simply state that Allen was not present on the first day of the conference, and that he arrived on the second day and accepted the designation of the conference. This would imply that he was not involved in the obvious politicking to get rid of Coker. Payne writes:

> On the 9th of April, 1816, an election took place for bishop, and Daniel Coker was elected on account of his superior education and talents. An objection was immediately made by the pure blacks, led by Jonathan Tudas, a friend *in council with Richard Allen*. This objection was on account of his color, his mother being an Englishwoman and his father a pure African. Daniel Coker, being a man of high feeling, resigned on the spot in favor of Richard Allen, who was then absent in the country, but arrived on the 10th, and hearing the facts of the case accepted the nomination to the bishopric. There is not a scrap of paper in existence relative to this important era of the A.M.E. Church. It was the desire of conciliating the opposing factions which led Bishop Allen later to name Morris Brown (who was not a black man) for the office of bishop, and the same cause led the latter to name Edward Waters (a dark man) for the same office. But the last-named bishop served, simply bearing the title without exercising any of the functions of the office.[28]

While some black preachers during slavery might have concentrated their sermons on life in the next world, they were not oblivious to delicate, political, personal matters of this world. Many of them were members of important hierarchical church structures, and it took the ingenuity of a most adept machine politician to survive and grow to a position of leadership in those structures. A serious disadvantage exists in our understanding of the earlier period, because as Payne points out, historical records of some important events are sparse, if indeed extant. But one can surmise from the available data that the black preachers were not totally preoccupied with preparing a place for themselves and their followers in the life hereafter. They spent more than a little time jockeying for positions of leadership within the churches and protecting those power positions once obtained. In other words, it is safe to conclude that while many of them emphasized the next world in their sermons, they also took care of personal, political, church-related relationships in this world. In the process of doing this, they were further developing leadership skills and organizational talents.

The point to be made here is that many ministers did not relate their religious teachings to the immediate, this-worldly problems of ending slavery. But they were concerned with issues on this earth which related to matters of intragroup relationship and the maintenance of vast church structures. Critics of the black preachers during slavery who charge that the preachers were dysfunctional to the black struggle and served essentially as "tools of the slave oppressors" have this role in mind in their criticism. They contend that a religion that did not frontally attack social and political injustices was an opiate of the people, and that those preachers who concerned themselves only with maintaining their individual leadership were self-seeking and parasites on the people. The same charge could be brought against many preachers today, but as we shall see, this by no means can be a blanket criticism.

Emphasis on This World and Abolition

It is certain that virtually every black movement before the Civil War that was connected with either abolition of slavery or the improvement of the conditions of free blacks had black preachers involved in its leadership. If they had the inclination—and very many did—their talents as orators and their skills in organization building made them natural leaders. Many were actively involved in the underground railroad that helped runaway slaves escape the South; [29] indeed, some were runaway slaves themselves. They were influential in starting schools for blacks, in the abolitionist organizations, in publishing ventures and in the black-convention movement that began in 1830. Black churches were frequently the only places in some Northern towns where abolitionist meetings could be held.[30]

In 1831, the Reverend Nat Turner attempted to lead a group of slaves in a violent revolt against slavery in Virginia, a revolt that resulted in the death of fifty-seven whites and one hundred blacks. This is one of the most publicized slave revolts in the history of the country. Turner, a slave, revealed in his confession how he had been commanded by God to lead the revolt.

> As I was praying one day at my plough, the Spirit spoke to me, saying, "Seek ye the Kingdom of Heaven, and all things shall be added unto you." . . . The Spirit that spoke to the prophets in former days. —And I was greatly astonished, and for two years prayed continually, whenever my duty would permit; and then again I had the same revelation, which fully confirmed me in the impression that I was ordained for some great purpose in the hands of the Almighty. Several years rolled round, in which many events occurred to strengthen me in this my belief.
> . . . And on the 12th of May, 1828, I heard a loud noise in the heavens, and the Spirit instantly appeared to me and said the Serpent was loosened, and Christ had laid down the yoke he had borne for the sins of men, and that I should take it on and fight against the Serpent, for the time was fast approaching when the first should be last and the last should be first. [When Nat Turner was asked by his interrogator in

jail, "Do you not find yourself mistaken now?" his answer was "Was not Christ crucified?"] And by signs in the heavens that it would make known to me when I should conceal it from the knowledge of men; and on the appearance of the sign (the eclipse of the sun, last February), I should arise and prepare myself, and slay my enemies with their own weapons.[31]

It quickly became known after the insurrection that Nat Turner was a preacher, and this fact caused many whites to conclude that black preachers, generally, were a disruptive force among and a bad influence on the slaves. They were seen as agitators, inciting to riot and rebellion. Several Southern states proceeded to enact laws either silencing black preachers altogether or severely restricting their ministerial activities. Virginia passed such a law in 1832. In 1833, Alabama enacted a law prohibiting blacks—free or slave—from preaching unless there were five respectable slave-holders present and only then when the preaching was authorized by a local religious society. A Georgia law passed in 1834 stipulated that no black could preach to more than seven persons at one time unless he was licensed by a judge and had received a certificate of approval from three ordained ministers.[32]

As could be expected, other laws were passed restricting the hours blacks could meet, defining meeting places, expelling free blacks from certain areas, and generally holding a tighter rein on preachers and their activities. These measures applied in the slave states, but in the North some black preachers continued to use their positions and pulpits to speak out forcefully against slavery.

Throughout the period from 1800 to the Civil War, black preachers advocated the total abolition of slavery. On the day the federal law prohibiting slave trade went into effect, January 1, 1808, the Reverend Peter Williams, Jr., spoke in the New York African Church:

Oh, God! we thank thee, that thou didst condescend to listen to the cries of Africa's wretched sons; and that thou didst interfere in their behalf. . . .

May the time speedily commence, when Ethiopia shall stretch forth her hands; when the sun of liberty shall beam replendent on the whole African race; and its genial influences, promote the luxuriant growth of knowledge and virtue.[33]

(As was pointed out earlier, he was later ordered by his white superiors in the Episcopal Church to remain silent on such issues, and he obeyed orders.)

The State of New York abolished slavery on July 4, 1827, and many blacks saw this as a hopeful sign of steady progress toward total abolition of slavery. A prominent black preacher in Albany, New York, the Reverend Nathaniel Paul of the First African Baptist Society, echoed the sentiments of many blacks when he spoke on July 5, 1827, of the inevitable emancipation of all peoples. Relying heavily on his faith in God, he spoke strongly of the basic equality of man—not only in the eyes of God, but in such matters as the ability to govern. This surely was a notion not shared by many persons at that time. It is also important to note that Reverend Paul did not confine his call for abolition to this country.

The progress of emancipation, though slow, is nevertheless certain: It is certain, because that God who has made of one blood all nations of men, and who is said to be no respecter of persons, has so decreed; I therefore have no hesitation in declaring from this sacred place, that not only throughout the United States of America, but throughout every part of the habitable world where slavery exists, it will be abolished. However great may be the opposition of those who are supported by the traffic, yet slavery will cease.

. . . I declare that slavery will be extinct; a universal

and not a partial emancipation must take place; nor is the period far distant.

. . . Did I believe that it would always continue, and that man to the end of time would be permitted with impunity to usurp the same undue authority over his fellow, I would disallow my allegiance or obligation I was under to my fellow creatures, or any submission that I owed to the laws of my country; I would deny the superintending power of divine providence in the affairs of this life; I would ridicule the religion of the Savior of the world, and treat as the worst of men the ministers of an everlasting gospel; I would consider my Bible as a book of false and delusive fables, and commit it to the flames; nay, I would still go farther; I would at once confess myself an atheist, and deny the existence of a holy God. But slavery will cease, and the equal rights of man will be universally acknowledged.

. . . We do well to remember, that every act of ours is more or less connected with the general cause of emancipation. Our conduct has an important bearing, not only on those who are yet in bondage in this country, but its influence is extended to the isles of India, and to every part of the world where the abomination of slavery is known. Let us then relieve ourselves from the odious stigma which some have long since cast upon us, that we were incapacitated by the God of nature, for the enjoyment of the rights of freemen, and convince them and the world that although our complexion may differ, yet we have hearts susceptible of feeling; judgment capable of discerning, and prudence sufficient to manage our affairs with discretion, and by example prove ourselves worthy the blessings we enjoy.[34]

This same Reverend Paul wrote a biting, sarcastic letter to a judge in New Haven, Connecticut, on August 29, 1833, denouncing the judge for sentencing a white lady, a Quaker, to jail. The lady, Prudence Crandall, had admitted black girls to her school. When the white students withdrew, she kept the school open to blacks. A mob wrecked the building, and the teacher was sentenced to jail by Judge Andrew T. Judson. Traveling in England at the time on an antislavery speaking tour, Reverend Paul wrote the judge from overseas:

> And believing that acts so patriotic, so republican, so Christian-like in their nature, as yours, against the unpardonable attempts of this fanatical woman, should not be confined to one nation or continent, but that the World should know them, and learn and profit thereby;—I have thought proper to do all in my power to spread your fame, that your works may be known at least throughout this country.
>
>   . . . And as I have been for some months past and still am engaged in traveling and delivering lectures upon the state of slavery as it exists in the United States, and the condition of the free people of color there, it will afford me an excellent opportunity of making this whole affair known; nor shall I fail to improve it.[35]

The black preacher then proceeded to promise that he intended to make the judge's name synonymous with that of Benedict Arnold's and that he would "make no charge for the service I may render you."

Black preachers during this period not only spoke forcefully, but some organized and acted. The Reverend Theodore S. Wright of New York helped form the New York Committee of Vigilance in 1835. Its purpose was to protect runaway slaves and to prevent the kidnaping of blacks to be sold into slavery. The first annual report of the Committee stated that as of January 16, 1837, a total of 335 blacks had been protected.[36]

Benjamin Quarles reports that all the blacks who were charter members of the American and Foreign Anti-Slavery Society (founded in May, 1840) were clergymen.[37] Five

were on the first executive committee: Samuel Cornish
(Presbyterian), Christopher Rush (A.M.E. Zion), George
Whipple (American Missionary Association), Charles B.
Ray (Congregationalist) and James W. C. Pennington
(Presbyterian). The fact that three different denominations
were represented among the group might well have been
an attempt to provide a broad representational base. This
sort of balancing has always been important in organizations attempting to incorporate large numbers of people.
And there is no reason to believe that black preachers were
not sensitive to these requirements.

The historical evidence seems to support the conclusion
that during slavery the idea of colonization did not receive
wide support from outspoken black preachers. For the
most part, the preachers who spoke out on conditions of
blacks sought the remedies of emancipation and an end to
discrimination, rather than colonization. The latter was
seen as an effort to get rid of free black people, and not
as a viable alternative to the institution of slavery. The
annual conventions begun in 1830, in which many ministers participated, occupied themselves not only with affairs of this life, but thought in terms of solving problems
in the context of society. Typical of the resolutions was
one passed at the fifth annual national convention held in
Philadelphia in 1835: "That the free people of color are
requested by this convention, to petition those state legis-
latures that have adopted the Colonization Society, to
abolish it. . . ."

From time to time, however, there were most assuredly
some black ministers who not only advocated that blacks
should leave, but did leave themselves. Reverend Daniel
Coker, who had lost out to Richard Allen as the first
A.M.E. bishop, left with eighty-six other free blacks and
settled in Sierra Leone in 1820, a move sponsored by the
American Colonization Society.[39] In his correspondence he

spoke of his intent "to give my life to bleeding, groaning, dark, benighted Africa," and of his belief that "it will be a great nation."

In examining historical records, one finds that some black preachers have been far harsher on their white counterparts than they have been on fellow black ministers, especially in the failure to condemn slavery. Seldom privately, and virtually never publicly, does one hear one black preacher condemn another as lacking in religious faith. Even when their views are diametrically opposed on social issues, one does not find a public debate among black preachers questioning the sincerity or integrity of one another. That is, they may take stands with which their fellow ministers do not agree, but they seldom, if ever, call into question one another's commitment to Christian or religious beliefs. They do not condemn each other as hypocrites who fail to teach the word of God. The historical evidence, especially during slavery, reveals, however, that a number of black preachers were severely critical of white ministers for failing to take strong stands against slavery.

At the Christian Anti-Slavery Convention in Cincinnati in April, 1850, Reverend Samuel Ringgold Ward criticized the white churches for defaulting on their biblical duties over the issue of slavery.[40] Many black ministers condemned the white churches for taking weak stands on slavery and for segregating black parishioners in many of their pews. These acts were seen as immoral. The Reverend James W. C. Pennington made the following comment at an antislavery convention in London in 1843: "If I meet my white brother minister in the street, he blushes to own me; meet him in our deliberative bodies, he gives me the go-by; meet him at the communion table, and he looks at me sideways." [41]

There may be a number of reasons why black ministers

leveled their strongest attacks against white churches and white ministers: Many of the whites theoretically professed a belief in abolition and, at times, even in the equality of all men; the blacks might have felt that if the white preachers took a more forceful and uncompromising position, positive results would ensue; they might have felt that those black preachers who were silent on the issue of slavery (or even opposed to abolition) were victims of the kind of pressure brought on the Reverend Peter Williams, Jr., by the bishops of the Episcopal Church.

There were times when the black preachers recognized that they should speak to the responsibilities of black people themselves. At the tenth annual conference of the western district of the A.M.E. Church in September, 1840, a set of resolutions was passed which spoke to the value of education, temperance and moral reform:

> That, whereas education is one of the principal means of creating in our minds those noble feelings which prompt us to the practice of piety, virtue, and temperance, and is calculated to elevate us above the condition of brutes, by assimilating us to the image of our Maker, we therefore recommend to all our preachers to enjoin undeviating attention to its promotion, and earnestly request all our people to neglect no opportunity of advancing it, by pledging ourselves to assist them as far as it is in our power. . . .
>
> That we hereby recommend to all our preachers, in their labors to promote the cause of temperance, to hold up the principle of total abstinence from (as a beverage) all intoxicating drinks . . .
>
> . . . that a sermon be preached, quarterly . . . by our preachers, on the subjects of temperance and moral reform; and the preacher in charge who neglects to attend to that duty, or see that it is attended to, shall be amenable to the next annual conference. . . .
>
> . . . that there be four sermons preached in the year,

in all our churches and congregations, for the purpose of encouraging the cause of education and Sabbath schools among our people. . . .[42]

It is not known if all A.M.E. preachers lived up to these resolutions, or if, failing to do so, they were called to answer before the conference. But the resolutions indicate the kinds of things the Church expected its black ministers to deal with. Their concerns were not to be entirely focused on the life hereafter.

Unquestionably, one of the most prominent, outspoken and uncompromising black preachers in the nineteenth century was the Reverend Henry Highland Garnet. Born in slavery in 1815 in Maryland, he escaped at the age of nine with his father, mother and sister to New York. After several years slave chasers captured his sister, and his parents were separated from him. For thirteen years he worked, went to school and studied theology. He was ordained a minister in the Presbyterian Church in 1842. The following year, at the annual National Negro Convention in Buffalo, he made one of the most memorable speeches in black history. Deciding deliberately to address himself to the slaves still in bondage, he issued a fervent call to them to rise up and resist their slave masters even to the point of death. He admonished that God would *not* reward those who accepted their bondage passively. "The forlorn condition in which you are placed, does not destroy your moral obligation to God. You are not certain of heaven, because you suffer yourselves to remain in a state of slavery." Thus he took a position quite opposite to that of earlier preachers such as Richard Allen. God did not require slaves to love and obey their masters. ". . . it is your solemn and imperative duty to use every means, both moral, intellectual, and physical that promises success." He reminded the slaves that *they* must strike the blow for freedom.

Garnet advised that the slaves should petition the slave owners to free them, and if this were not successful ". . . for ever after cease to toil for the heartless tyrants." *A general strike!* Perhaps they would be killed.

> You had better all die—*die immediately,* than live slaves and entail your wretchedness upon your posterity. If you would be free in this generation, here is your only hope. However much you and all of us may desire it, there is not much hope of redemption without the shedding of blood. If you must bleed, let it all come at once—rather die freemen, than live to be slaves.

Although he did not call for open, violent revolt, many delegates to the convention understood his words in this vein. Frederick Douglass, the famous black abolitionist, could not endorse the speech because there was in it "too much physical force." [43] In fact, a careful reading of Garnet's speech will reveal that he was calling for mass resistance in the form of a strike. "Brethren, arise, arise! Strike for your lives and liberties. . . . Let your motto be resistance! resistance! Resistance. No oppressed people have ever secured their liberty without resistance." At the end of his speech, he left the door open for the slaves to pursue his call by various ways which suited their particular situation. "What kind of resistance you had better make, you must decide by the circumstances that surround you, and according to the suggestion of expediency."

The convention failed by one vote to endorse the speech, but Garnet remained throughout his career—which ended in 1881 on his death in Africa as a minister resident in Liberia—a militant spokesman for equal rights for black people. He frequently debated Frederick Douglass on the course the black struggle should take. Garnet developed plans for organizing an African Colonization Society. Douglass disagreed with him. Lerone Bennett observes the consequences of their split: "After Douglass abandoned the Garrisonian program, the two men were not divided on substantive matters. But the clash continued, to the detriment of a unified black front. Worse, white men were able to pit Douglass against Garnet, thereby diminishing the force of both." [44]

Slavery was finally ended as a consequence of the Civil War. Throughout the nearly 250 years of its existence in this country, black preachers played roles that covered the spectrum; from those like the Reverend Jupiter Hammon who admonished the slaves to look for happiness in the next world only; to those such as the Reverend Richard Allen who condemned slavery but counseled the slaves to love and obey their masters, because God would take care of the evil institution of human bondage; to those like the Reverend Daniel Coker who advocated and personally pursued black colonization in Africa; to the Reverend Nat Turner who felt commanded by God to lead a violent revolt against slavery; to men like the Reverend Henry Highland Garnet. The diversity among the black preachers exists to this time, and therefore makes simplistic conclusions unwise, if not, in fact, erroneous. Black preachers have always been pacifiers, passive resisters and vigilantes. And each type has had, and continues to have to this day, substantial following in the black communities. They have this in common: They have all been leaders of their people—a people needing comfort, instruction, encouragement and guidance. At some point during slavery, the various preachers filled, in their own ways, these needs. Even when the slave preacher was not a revolutionary, the evidence indicates that his next-worldly message at times provided a momentary respite from the hardships of the day. And even when the black preachers had to "sing their songs in a whisper and pray in a whisper"—at times when a little noise would have been a welcome relief—their people went to them and listened to them.

For a number of reasons and in many ways, the black preacher during the traumatic period of slavery had, indeed, many witnesses.

III

Many Pastors,
Many Pews

Most black Americans who profess a religious affiliation are Baptists or Methodists. This reflects the fact that these two denominations were more active than the other denominations in proselyting among black slaves. Revivals and camp meetings were numerous at particular times, especially during the latter half of the eighteenth century and at the turn of the nineteenth century. Professor Melville J. Herskovits suggests that the attraction of the Baptists was related to certain features in the Negro's African heritage. He has stated: "The importance of baptism in the ritual practices of Negro Christians has often been commented upon. It is not unreasonable to relate the strength of adherence to this practice to the great importance of the river-cults in West Africa, particularly in view of the fact that . . . river-cult priests were sold into slavery in great numbers." [1]

Professor E. Franklin Frazier is not impressed by this explanation. He writes: "The proselyting activities of the Baptists and Methodists provide an adequate explanation of the fact that the majority of the Negroes are members of the Baptist church. . . . The Negro slaves seemingly from the beginning of their residence in the United States took over the religious beliefs and rituals to which they were exposed." [2]

In addition, the Baptist and Methodist churches had a greater degree of autonomy than churches in other denominations, and it was easier for blacks to become preachers, and therefore leaders, in Baptist and Methodist churches. This situation has persisted over the years. Frazier has also concluded that the form of emotional worship characteristic of the Baptists and Methodists was a factor in attracting large numbers of blacks to those denominations. He says:

> Then there were other factors in the situation that caused the slaves to respond to the forms of religious expression provided by the Baptists and Methodists. As we have indicated, the slaves who had been torn from their homeland and kinsmen and friends, and whose cultural heritage was lost, were isolated and broken men, so to speak. In the emotionalism of the camp meetings and revivals some social solidarity, even if temporary, was achieved, and they were drawn into a union with their fellow men.[3]

Today, memberships, number of churches and number of pastors are largest in the Baptist and Methodist denominations. There are approximately 9,668,000 members of Baptist churches in the three black national Baptist organizations: National Baptist Convention, U.S.A., Inc. (five million), National Baptist Convention of America (2,668,000), and Progressive National Baptist Convention, Inc. (2,000,000). The number of churches in the three groups are 26,000, 11,398, and 1,450 respectively. The National Baptist Convention, U.S.A., Inc., was formed in 1895 in Atlanta, and there are now approximately 27,500 ministers. There are 7,598 ministers in the National Baptist Convention of America.[4] Approximately 1,000 ministers belong to the Progressive National Baptist Convention.

These figures, of necessity, are approximate, because there may well be smaller Baptist churches, especially in rural areas, that are neither affiliated with the national bodies nor reported in the compiled statistics. The Baptists do not have the highly centralized ecclesiastical structure of some other denominations. Thus it is easier for a person to come along and set up his own church and start preaching.

Some larger Baptist churches will have several assisting ministers on the full-time staff, headed by the pastor of the church. These ministers are in charge of various departments within the church. In smaller churches, such duties are frequently performed by volunteer laymen. Some younger ministers just starting their ministerial careers seek positions as assisting ministers, as a means of serving an apprenticeship for a few years before they begin to preach for parishes of their own. Thus one will find an Assistant Minister for Youth Work, an Assistant Minister for Community Affairs, an Assistant Minister for the Sick and Shut-in, an Assistant Minister for Missionary Work, and so on.

The first black Baptist national body was organized in 1867 as the Consolidated American Baptist Convention and lasted thirteen years, until 1880. Three groups grew out of this structure: the Foreign Mission Baptist Convention (1880), the American National Baptist Convention (1880), and the American National Educational Baptist Convention (1893). One overall organization, the National Baptist Convention of the U.S.A., brought these groups together in 1895.

In the National Baptist Convention of America (1915), the Progressive National Baptist Convention, Inc. (1961), and two Methodist denominations, there are more churches than ministers. (In the A.M.E. Church, there are 5,878 churches, 5,878 ministers and 1.5 million members.) The A.M.E. Zion Church has 4,083 churches, 2,400 ministers and 770,000 members. There are 1,792 ministers for 2,523 C.M.E. churches and 444,493 members. In some of these churches, as in many smaller independent churches, one preacher is shared by as many as three or four other churches. He will preach at each church on a given Sunday in the month. This was and still is a prevalent practice in the rural South. In some instances, a pastor will hold regular services at as many as three churches on one Sunday, beginning with an eleven o'clock service and ending several miles away, in another county, at a seven o'clock service in the evening. In one rural Alabama church with a congregation of approximately twenty, one church elder described the procedure there:

> We will have service here at Shorter [Alabama] around seven this evening—whenever the pastor can get here. He has some churches to go to over in Montgomery County earlier today.

These kinds of churches are small, with memberships usually around fifty or less. His primary function is to preach a sermon. He is, therefore, much less involved in the intimate lives of the people than a minister who lives in the community and pastors one church, unless he happens to live reasonably close by. There are occasions when such a minister will be asked to counsel or to mediate a church, community or family problem—more frequently the last. This problem will be waiting for him when he visits the church. In many ways it is similar to the judge "riding circuit." One preacher in rural Alabama said:

> Oh sure, I spend time with my people. If they tell me that they want me to talk to so-and-so, maybe a boy or girl who is off on the wrong path, I make it my busi-

ness to do that when I go to that church. Even if it
holds me up, and I'm late getting to the next place.

This minister is normally paid no regular salary, but
he receives a donation taken at one of the collections during service. (The general practice is to announce the
amount collected with each passing of the plate.) More
frequently than not, because the members are usually
quite poor, he makes little more than his expenses. He
usually has other, full-time employment during the week.

Obviously, such ministers do not participate to a great
extent in the political, social or economic activities of the
members through the church. He is not around long
enough, and it is not expected of him. His relationship is
essentially one of "bringing the Word of the Lord," and
the sermon generally is one admonishing the parishioners
to live a Christian life so that they can go to heaven when
they die.

In such churches, a considerable part of the worshiping
is conducted by deacons and elders who lead devotional
services on those Sundays when the minister is not sched-
uled to appear or on his Sunday until he arrives.

There are no data compiled on the number of such
black churches and ministers in the country. One of the
best current sources for gaining information on the number and size of these churches is the new black elected
official increasingly common in many Southern counties.
This person in all likelihood has canvassed the county
and has come to know exactly where each little church is,
whether it has a permanent or circuit preacher and what
the approximate size of the congregation is. He was not
a resource available prior to the late 1960's and, of course,
he is a result of the increased politicization of the blacks in
recent years. (In doing the research for this book, one of
the most helpful persons in rural Macon County, Alabama,
was the newly elected black Circuit Court Clerk, Mr.
James Hopkins. He knew the location of many black

churches not on the main thoroughfare, as well as know-ing which ministers were politically active.)

Black membership in the Roman Catholic Church stands at roughly 703,000, which is virtually a threefold increase since World War II. The number of black priests is between 160 and 170, and there is one black Roman Catholic bishop. In 1967, *The Negro Almanac* [5] indicated that in ten dioceses [6] listed as "Negro Missions and Par-ishes—1965," there were 88,784 Catholics, fifty-four churches and seventy-five priests.[7]

There are about twenty-four independent black churches and religious organizations for which data are available as to the number of separate congregations and the size of membership, but there are no figures on the number of black ministers serving these churches.

Church *(date in parenthesis is date of organization)*	*Approximate number of churches*	*Approximate number of members*
The African Orthodox Church (1921)	25–30*	6,000*
The African Union First Colored Methodist Protestant Church, Inc. (1805)	30*	5,000*
The Apostolic Overcoming Holy Church of God (1919)	300*	75,000*
Christ's Sanctified Holy Church (1903)	30	600*
The Church of Christ, Holiness, U.S.A. (1896)	159	9,289

* Estimated figures.

Church (date in parenthesis is date of organization)	Approximate number of churches	Approximate number of members
The Church of God and Saints of Christ (1896)	217	38,127
The Church of God in Christ (1895)	4,500	425,000
The Church of the Living God (1889)	300	45,320
The Churches of God, Holiness (1914)	32	25,600
The Negro Churches of the Cumberland Presbyterian Church (1869)	121	30,000
The Fire Baptized Holiness Church (1898)	53	988
The Free Christian Zion Church of Christ (1905)	742	22,260
The House of God, Which Is The Church of the Living God, The Pillar and Ground of the Truth, Inc. (1918)	107	2,350
The Independent A.M.E. Denomination (1907)	12* (1940 figure)	1,000* (1940 figure)
The Kodesh Church of Immanuel (1929)	9*	562*

* Estimated figures.

Church (date in parenthesis is date of organization)	Approximate number of churches	Approximate number of members
The National Baptist Evangelical Life and Soul Saving Assembly of U.S.A. (1921)	264	57,674
The National David Spiritual Temple of Christ Church Union, Inc. (1921)	—	40,000
The National Primitve Baptist Convention of the U.S.A. (1907)	12,196	1,523,000
The Reformed Methodist Union Episcopal Church	60	5,000
The Reformed Zion Union Apostolic Church (1869)	50	16,000
Triumph the Church and Kingdom of God in Christ (1902)	430	48,500
The Union American Methodist Episcopal Church (1813)	256	27,560
The United Free Will Baptist Church (1870)	836	100,000
The United Holy Church of America, Inc. (1886)	470	28,980

* Estimated figures.

A number of these organizations are offshoots from the larger Baptist and Methodist denominations. In some instances, a single minister left his earlier affiliation and started his own religious movement. The above figures do not include the myriad small cults and sects found especially in storefronts or apartments in the urban Northern areas. It is virtually impossible to compile accurate statistics on these groups, inasmuch as some of them are no more than small, one-man, almost private operations with a regular following of perhaps twenty to forty—or fewer.

More than forty years ago, Professor Ira De A. Reid severely criticized these kinds of religious operations in Harlem in an article entitled "Let Us Prey!"

> The third group comprises those churches whose rent is paid by the pastor or some charitable member at whose home the services are held, with or without the permission of the landlord. The pastor assumes all responsibility for rent, light, and heat, as well as his salary, and receives *pro tanto* all incoming collections. The pastor of one such church is a student in one of the local schools, and from his church (which is conducted in the front room of his house) he derives enough money to defray all of his expenses. The church is nondenominational. The pastor boasts that he is not bound to any organized body and simply "preaches Jesus." His seats are chairs rented from a neighboring undertaker. He conducts his services on such days as he feels disposed mentally and indisposed financially. To this gentleman of the cloth—he is an ordained minister—the church is a legitimate business.[8]

These operations still exist, but there is no satisfactory way of getting an accurate count of their number or size. Many are ephemeral, not intended to be anything more than a temporary livelihood for the minister. They are, in essence, a hustle. And of course one would not expect the hustler to divulge too much, if any, information about his game. Professor Reid noted the high turnover of these kinds of places:

> In this group of churches there were fifty meeting in places that had outlived their usefulness as homes or places of business. These places rarely if ever seat fifty persons at the utmost, and are poorly lighted and ventilated. They are chiefly immediate neighborhood affairs, support depending upon the activity of the pastor in securing members from the surrounding apartments and tenements. It is because of this fact that the turnover among these churches is very high. They are forced to follow their members, secure new ones, or go out of business. Six weeks after the preliminary list of the churches was made seven of the churches previously listed could not be found.[9]

In spring, 1971, a cursory survey was made in central Harlem, attempting to determine the extent to which such activity still prevailed. Contacts were made largely through word of mouth. One minister printed leaflets and distributed them in front of the apartment the morning of the church service (which was to be held Wednesday evening) announcing time and place. Five such operations were found through this random technique. Three of the five had been meeting rather consistently once a week since the previous October; two had recently started. By late May only two were still holding services. At no time did the sessions contain more than twenty-five persons, and one third of this number were children under ten years of age, frequently babes in arms. The various congregations were overwhelmingly female, and the preacher in all five cases was male. "Business drops off when the weather gets better," one minister stated. "People stay outdoors more." This same man, the only one of the five who consented to an interview, defended his actions against charges of "taking the people" by stating: "I provide a service for people. If I take them anywhere, it's to God. I'm not holding up anybody, hitting them over the head, making them come in here. I preach the Word of God, and they're comforted by that. That's more than you can say for some of these so-called big-time name preachers." He indicated that his average collection was ten dollars a service, which usually lasted anywhere from one hour to two hours. "And you can't get rich off of that. If I wanted to get rich, I wouldn't be doing this. You can believe. Some people are always trying to tear down somebody, just because you don't have a big new church building and all. But that doesn't bother me any. I just help people see God's way."

Another major religious movement among black Americans is the Nation of Islam (the Black Muslims). There are no available, definitive statistics on the size of this group. The first major study of the organization was done by Professor C. Eric Lincoln, published in 1961.[10] He put the membership at 100,000 throughout the country. He stated at that time: "The Movement is growing rapidly, and it is nationwide; in December, 1960, there were sixty-nine temples or missions in twenty-seven states from California to Massachusetts and Florida." Lincoln indicated that "some estimates would triple that figure."

Another exhaustive study of the group, by Professor E. U. Essien-Udom in his book *Black Nationalism* in 1962, made the following observation:

> Observers have estimated the membership at between 10,000 and 250,000. One writer has said that one Negro in every 300 is a "registered" Muslim. None of them really knows. Muhammad himself has claimed a total of "half a million believers." In November, 1958, a source close to Muhammad said that there were over

3,000 registered Muslims, over 15,000 believers, and nearly 50,000 sympathizers. Another informant estimated registered membership at 12,000; and in January, 1960, still another estimated it at 5,000. The lowest number offered by any officer or member was 3,000 and the highest was 12,000. We estimate, after checking and rechecking as carefully as possible, that there are at present between 5,000 and 15,000 registered followers, at least 50,000 believers, and a much larger number of sympathizers.[11]

These figures are little more than a decade old. There has been no more knowledge gained on the size of the group since then. "Those who know," Malcolm X once said, "don't say. And those who say, don't know."

The Muslims are first and foremost a religious movement. The Nation of Islam is not a political or civil rights organization. The members believe that Allah (God) appeared in Detroit in July, 1930, in the person of Mr. W. Fard Muhammad, who stated that he came from the Holy City of Mecca. And he proclaimed his mission to be to achieve "freedom, justice and equality" for all black people of North America. He was at first a door-to-door salesman in Detroit's poor black neighborhoods, and subsequently organized a Temple which grew rapidly. The present spiritual leader of the group, Elijah Muhammad, is considered the Messenger of Allah.

Muhammad teaches that white, Western civilization is doomed, and that black people should work to separate themselves from white society. The group's statement of Belief reads, in part:

> We believe this is the time in history for the separation of the so-called Negroes and the so-called white Americans. . . .
> We believe that the offer of integration is hypocritical and is made by those who are trying to deceive the

black peoples into believing that their 400-year-old open enemies of freedom, justice and equality are, all of a sudden, their "friends." Furthermore, we believe that such deception is intended to prevent black people from realizing that the time in history has arrived for the separation from the whites of this nation.

Thus, the Muslims want to establish a separate state either on this continent or elsewhere, and they believe that the American government is "obligated to provide such land and that the area must be fertile and minerally rich."

Professor C. Eric Lincoln has described the group's attitude toward black Christian preachers:

The black Christian preacher is the white man's most effective tool for keeping the so-called Negroes pacified and controlled, for he tells convincing lies against nature as well as against God.[12]

Richard 25X is a black man in Harlem studying to become a minister in the Nation of Islam. As a child he attended the A.M.E. Church, and he recalls his Sunday-school experiences as "a big joke." "They don't teach you anything," he stated, "but foolishness." He was turned off by the intense emotionalism and shouting, and he compared the church services to a Sunday matinee, a kind of entertainment and sideshow.

After the A.M.E. Church he became affiliated with various black nationalist organizations, stating that he had "a desire to better my people." Lynchings of blacks in the South affected him, and he remembers having intense feelings of wanting "to get even." Such groups as the Black African Pioneer Movement attracted him, but not for long. He found a rather low level of morality among the nationalists. He stated: "I noticed that some young girls would join who were virgins, and the leaders would deflower them. I did not like that."

Thus he continued to search for a group consistent with his ideas of morality and racial struggle. In the early 1960's he saw a poster in Harlem announcing a meeting at which Elijah Muhammad was to speak. This started him thinking seriously about the Nation of Islam. He recalled, "I said to myself, I bet this old-timer is on the ball." He attended the meeting but was not impressed at first. He remembers being disappointed with what he then considered to be Elijah Muhammad's inability to speak clearly and distinctly.

Richard 25X, then Richard Grant, was in the distributing business, and he serviced three hundred newsstands. He did not join the Nation of Islam immediately, but he decided to start distributing the organization's newspaper, *Muhammad Speaks,* to the newsstands. After two years of attending Muslim meetings, he decided to join.

Several things drew him to the group. He liked the fact that "there were no brothers hitting on the women like in the other organizations." He was also impressed by the philosophy of defending one's self against attack. "I never did like the philosophy of don't hit back," he said. And in the Nation of Islam he could see a group of highly disciplined black people organizing themselves for group advancement.

He stopped drinking liquor, eating pork and smoking reefers. And he notes, "I just felt good inside."

He joined the organization about the time of the split with Malcolm X, and he stated that he decided he would stay in the Nation of Islam and support Elijah Muhammad. Then and now he has unquestioning faith in the wisdom and integrity of the leader, and he confirms that by saying: "I'm like a diehard. You can't do anything with me. Some people you can approach with a white woman. And you can buy off some people with money, but the only thing that will stop me from supporting the Nation is death."

He credits Elijah Muhammad with contributing to his overcoming his fear of white people. One example was his decision to sell *Muhammad Speaks* among whites on a crowded, predominantly white street corner. He frequently sold the newspaper in front of Macy's department store on Thirty-fourth Street in Manhattan, and he chose to do this alone in order to overcome his fears. He did not know what reactions he would encounter from whites, but it was important to him to do this.

In the spring of 1972 he completed six months in a Muslim ministry class. The classes consisted of studying the lessons of Elijah Muhammad and mastering a "problem book." But this is only the first step toward becoming a minister. He is still considered a student minister. His next task is to begin to hold classes for non-members, to teach them the lessons he has learned. He will try to develop regular followers and then take them to the Muslim Temple in Harlem where an appointed Muslim minister will begin to teach the potential recruits.

Only Elijah Muhammad can appoint ministers, and if Richard 25X is recommended by his minister, he might receive such an appointment.

Characteristic of members of the Nation of Islam, he refers to his time before joining as "being in the grave." He now considers his life to have begun, and becoming a minister in the organization would be the highest goal he could attain. Short of achieving that status, he insists that he will continue to develop his distribution and other possible businesses toward the sole end of donating the money to the growth of the Nation of Islam.

In the early 1960's the most prominent spokesman for the Muslims was Malcolm X. Like many other members, he was recruited while in prison. He had spent his early years as a young man pursuing a life of crime. He became the most articulate supporter of Elijah Muhammad, and he developed a charismatic appeal among some black followers which was equaled at the time only by the appeal of another black preacher, Martin Luther King, Jr. Malcolm X, a high school dropout, put himself under the tutelage of Elijah Muhammad. He was able, because of his background, to relate to the most oppressed element in the black community. He had been where they were; he spoke their language and understood their life-style. In many ways, he embodied the total black experience, and it was precisely these qualities that contributed to his ability to communicate with and attract many to the Nation of Islam.

But, beginning in late 1963, a split developed between Malcolm X and Elijah Muhammad. The facts and interpretations vary, but it is clear that the tensions were both ideological and personal. Malcolm X was suspended in December, 1963, and in March, 1964, he formed his own organizations, Muslim Mosque and the Organization of Afro-American Unity.

In meetings of the Nation of Islam today one might hear an occasional reference to Malcolm X as "the hypocrite" who became overly enamored with the national publicity and attempted to ignore the teachings of Elijah Muhammad. In his *Autobiography,* Malcolm indicated that he was disappointed with the policy of the Nation of Islam not to become involved in political action. He wrote:

> If I harbored any personal disappointment whatsoever it was that privately I was convinced that our Nation of Islam could be an even greater force in the American black man's overall struggle—if we engaged in more *action.* By that, I mean I thought privately that we should have amended, or relaxed, our general non-engagement policy. I felt that, wherever black people committed themselves, in the Little Rocks and the

> Birminghams and other places, militantly disciplined Muslims should also be there—for all the world to see, and respect, and discuss.[13]

There was another difference between Malcolm X and the Nation of Islam that developed after his split with the organization. He came to view some whites as sincere and not all of them as "devils." He persisted in his views that blacks should organize their own groups, exclusive of whites, but he also felt that there was a crucial role for whites to play in the struggle for justice:

> Where the really sincere white people have got to do their "proving" of themselves is not among the black *victims,* but out on the battle lines of where America's racism really *is*—and that's in their own home communities; America's racism is among their own fellow whites. That's where the sincere whites who really mean to accomplish something have got to work.[14]

Malcolm's transformation really began with his pilgrimage to Mecca in 1964. It was on that trip that he became aware of what he called the "color-blindness" of the Islamic faith. He wrote:

> The *color-blindness* of the Muslim world's religious society and the *color-blindness* of the Muslim world's human society: these two influences had each day been making a greater impact, and an increasing persuasion against my previous way of thinking.[15]

> America needs to understand Islam, because this is one religion that erases from its society the race problem.[16]

Malcolm X never got the chance to develop his newfound religion among black people in America. On February 21, 1965, at a meeting in Harlem he was shot to death by several black men whose affiliations and motivations are still unknown. It is certain that he was in a highly transitional period in his life, and precisely where it would have led him is impossible to guess. But in a sense his entire life was one of constant transition. In his brief thirty-nine years he had experienced a number of careers: hustler, pimp, laborer, prisoner, teacher, minister, leader. He was constantly struggling and changing and adapting. In many ways this is the story of black people, and it is appropriate that that story should be reflected in the life of one of their most dynamic preachers in modern times.

IV

Education and the Ministry

The Education of Black Preachers

In later chapters of this book, interviews with seven black preachers are presented. All seven have attended college, six have graduated from college and six have some amount of formal religious training. Four of the seven have received a seminary degree. The reader should not assume, however, that these men have the average or typical educational backgrounds of most black preachers. The opposite is the case. Dr. Harry V. Richardson, as quoted earlier, has stated: "Recent figures show that only one out of fifteen men entering the ministry has had seminary training. In other words, 92 percent of the men entering the Negro ministry each year are professionally unprepared." [1]

The relative lack of formal as well as seminary education has been a serious concern of some black ministers and lay people for some time. Reports of conferences of the A.M.E. Church dating back to before the Civil War are fraught with resolutions calling for more attention to this problem. In spite of the fact that the emphasis of early black education—after the Civil War—was on the training of ministers, one study in the 1920's found that,

for the most part, such training had been inferior to that
of other departments in black schools.[2] The earlier leaders
of the black church were found to be better educated in
comparison to black laymen than latter-day ministers compared to present laymen. Reverend W. A. Daniel notes:

> Contrary to popular belief, men like George Liele,
> Andrew Bryan, Richard Allen and others, who founded
> the Negro church before the Civil War, were men of
> some education. They were not as well educated as are
> the present leaders in the Negro church; but they were
> better educated as compared with the laymen of their
> day than are the present leaders as compared with the
> laymen of to-day.[3]

The problem is aggravated by two situations: standards
for licensing ministers and the tradition of the "call to
the ministry." The standards for being licensed to preach
were and are lower than those to practice other professions
such as law, medicine, dentistry and teaching. This has not
motivated some prospective ministers to put as much emphasis on formal training as would normally be the case.
Some recognize and believe that the ministry is a profession in the same sense as other professions, but the field
itself has not insisted on it, generally, in recruiting people
into it. Daniel also says:

> Because of the low standards for licensing ministers
> as compared with the standards for licensing men in
> other professions, the candidates for the ministry are
> not as easily convinced of the necessity for thorough
> preparation as are the candidates for professions with
> higher licensing requirements.[4]

While it is difficult and unwise to generalize, it is accurate to state that in some places the seminary or theological
department has not had academic prestige comparable
to that of other departments or schools in a particular

university. This was certainly the case at Lincoln University in Pennsylvania, before it decided in the late 1950's to discontinue its seminary altogether. The school was founded in 1854 as Ashmun Institute by a white Presbyterian minister, and the name was changed to Lincoln University in 1866. Schools of medicine and law were discontinued decades ago. The seminary, which was under the control of the General Assembly of the Presbyterian Church, U.S.A., apparently was one of the stronger components of the university until after World War II. In the 1950's, however, the seminary began to acquire a reputation on the campus as a place for the weaker students, those unable to meet the more rigorous academic requirements in other departments. (The university, incidentally, had and has a very high reputation as a four-year liberal-arts college. Many prominent black men—it was basically not co-ed until the mid-1960's—did their undergraduate work there: Thurgood Marshall, Langston Hughes, Kwame Nkrumah.) Students who failed in their studies in the admittedly more demanding natural, biological and social sciences could transfer to the seminary and be "given a ride." In addition to becoming virtually a cause for ridicule, the seminary was receiving fewer and fewer students each year. Consequently, in 1959, the seminary was discontinued.

One professor, not in the seminary faculty, said, "It just became a laughingstock. No one respected it. You know, Lincoln has a reputation of having a very good undergraduate program, especially in pre-med and pre-law. It got to be: 'If you can't do anything else, then preach. But first go to the seminary.' We just couldn't have that kind of thing. Why, there were guys over here making C's and D's and almost flunking out who would go over there and come out almost cum laude. That was just ridiculous. So I'm glad they closed it down."

Closing a seminary was one alternative. Another was to try to improve the quality of education. In addition, at one time and perhaps today, there was also the attitude that *some* training was better than *no* training. Historian W. A. Daniel commented:

> . . . for the philosophy of the denominational bodies, which determines the entrance standards of their theological departments, is to the effect that a poorly prepared man will take some rural or slum church, which a man better prepared will not take, and will bring it up to a level at which a man better prepared will be willing to take charge and further improve it. We must have somebody for every church. "Poor leadership is better than no leadership at all." It is further urged that since some men are going to preach anyhow, it is better to do *something* for these men than to let them go wholly unprepared.[5]

He stated that the first argument was advanced especially by the Methodist groups, while the second was associated primarily with the Baptists. There is evidence, however, that over the last few years those theological schools that have remained in existence training future black preachers have attempted to improve the quality of the education provided. These schools have revised their curriculum, increased their libraries and improved their faculties.

Another phenomenon operating against strong emphasis on formal training has been the "call to the ministry." A man who is called is one chosen and prepared by God for the responsibilities of being a good preacher. (Reverend Henry Lewis discusses this subject at length in Chapter VIII.) One Baptist deacon in Alabama commented:

> No man will ever be able to take a major role in the works of the church without being divinely called. I'm not a fighter against education, but education alone will not do the job. This has been tried down through

the ages. We must have a divine call. We must have the divine guidance of God. And we must have a sense of direction from God.

You see, to me, you can't read enough to be saved. To me, you can't understand enough to be saved. To me, you'll never know enough to be saved. That won't save you. The Apostle Paul, the Dean of the New Testament Church, stated: "By faith, through grace, ye are saved and not of yourself."

This kind of statement is normally accompanied by a strong reaffirmation of the value of a formal education. But one gets the impression when hearing it that of the two, education and the divine call, the latter is far more important and indispensable. Noting that "some conscientious men hesitate to enter the ministry" because they have not experienced the call, Reverend W. A. Daniel also concluded:

The "call-to-the-ministry" belief, to which the students have been accustomed in their home communities, and which is held by most of the ministerial students, tends to minimize the importance of a high-grade theological education, and to discount its value.[6]

Several black denominations, churches and ministers have for some time voiced a deep concern that the ministry should be highly educated, without sacrificing its commitment to spirituality. In fact, they have felt that the former helps to articulate and pursue the latter more efficiently and intelligently. The records of the A.M.E. Church reveal this continuing concern.

At the sixteenth General Conference in 1880 in St. Louis, Bishop T. M. D. Ward preached the Quadrennial Sermon on the subject "The Shepherd and His Flock." He emphasized the importance of an educated ministry:

Brain power will be supreme. Encourage learning and you will live; despise it and you will die. An en-

lightened ministry, whose talents and calling have been
consecrated to God, will make an intelligent, large-
hearted Church. "Like priest, like people." We should
select books that contain within as small a compass as
possible the pith and marrow of the best authors upon
such subjects which most interest and concern us. No
man can learn everything, but what any other man has
done we can do. Master whatever you take in hand. A
knowledge of the classics, and especially of mathematics,
will be great aids in the interpretation of the doctrines
of the gospel.[7]

The view was taken that men who were "called" should
be subsequently "prepared." This was *their* responsibility,
inasmuch as their parishioners, busily engaged in secular
affairs, would not have the time to acquire the special
knowledge of Christianity. And one bishop, L. J. Coppin,
in an address before the twenty-fifth General Conference
in Philadelphia in 1916, observed that much damage could
be done by an inadequate education, thus disagreeing with
the proposition that it was better to have a poorly trained
minister than one not trained at all. Bishop Coppin spoke
on "An Efficient Ministry." Even in his choice of the term
"efficient," and in his explanation for choosing it, he indicated the difficulties with the word "educated." In a
sense, he appeared to be trying to dispel any notions of
elitism—that the minister would be out of touch and tune
with his people—while at the same time attempting to preserve for the ministry the special province of its being a
profession.

We have used the word "efficient" in order to avoid the
too often misused and misunderstood word "educated."
By an efficient ministry is meant one that is in every
way prepared for the responsible task of leadership in
the Church of God. That the "Priest's lips should keep
knowledge," is a truism too self-evident to require repe-
tition. In this day of light and knowledge, of free and

MEDIA SERVICES   142929
EVANSTON TOWNSHIP HIGH SCHOOL
EVANSTON, ILLINOIS 60204

liberal education, of schools of every description, of a
public educational system that begins with the kinder-
garten and goes step by step to the university, making
it possible for all to possess a degree of enlightenment
for every vocation in life, it would be no less than a
crime, not to say sacrilege, for him who has the care
of souls to be content to remain ignorant as it relates
to the prevalent learning of the day.

Men cannot obtain certificates to pursue the learned
professions until they have qualified themselves for the
work. But in too many instances persons are found in
ministerial garb who have not mastered the elements
of an education in their mother tongue. Others there
are who have simply acquired enough to make them
appear ridiculous by the misuse of what they have but
imperfectly learned. Still another class will, with dip-
lomatic cowardice, denounce learning as being repug-
nant to spirituality. By a strange inclination on the part
of humanity to be by nature perverse, these unprepared
leaders can summon a following, at least for a time, but
much to the detriment of enlightened Christianity and
all that makes for true progress in morals and religion.
Therefore, a reasonable literary standard must be maintained for the Christian ministry—a standard which will
enable the minister to profitably serve all classes that
constitute the sum of humanity.[8]

On more than one occasion, the bishops of the A.M.E.
Church expressed concern that the lay members of the
church would be educated beyond the general educational
level of the ministry. This would be detrimental to the
church and to the ministry. The parishioners would lose
respect for the preachers. The authority of the preachers
would be undermined, and there would be a general fall-
ing off of church membership. Public educational systems
were growing, exposing more and more people to an education. There was considerable fear that there was not a

simultaneous growth of theological schools to provide a trained ministry for a congregation that would inevitably demand such. An increasingly educated parish would demand an increasingly educated pastorate.

In 1904, Bishop James A. Handy told the twenty-second General Conference assembled in Chicago:

> Our public school system, designed to insure the enlightenment of the masses, to say nothing of the influence of the higher institutions of learning, creates an imperative demand for an educated ministry. No thoughtful and observant person can gainsay that the pew is advancing in intelligence. This fact is emphasized by the presence of the schoolmaster in every part of the land. If the Church would win victories which are within the reach of its activities, it must see to it that the pulpit not only keeps pace with the pew but is in advance of it.
>
> . . . We do not mean to combat the proposition that the Church should aid in advancing the general enlightenment of the people, but we nevertheless affirm, that in our opinion, the first duty of the Church is to educate its ministry.[9]

And then, four years later, in 1908, at the twenty-third General Conference in Norfolk, Virginia, Bishop W. B. Derrick repeated the admonition when he stated that each year educational institutions were graduating "cultured young men and women." The advance of "culture" in the pews meant the need to keep pace with the "equal advancement of culture in the pulpit." [10]

The fear was that the ministry would be outstripped by the followers who would be more literate and generally better educated. That has not been a substantial problem in recent years. One finds that, for the most part, the congregation is either satisfied with the educational level of its pastor, or the pastor normally has more years of formal education than the average layman in the congregation. It would be an oddity to find a church where many or most of the parishioners were high-school graduates with some college education and the minister had not finished high school. Such a church would probably not tolerate a minister who split infinitives, used double negatives and generally did not have a reasonably good command of the English language.

In addition, there is virtually no instance where the congregation is dissatisfied with the minister because of what it considers to be his lack of knowledge of the teachings of the Bible. Great theological debates do not occur within the church anyway, and it is quite sufficient that the minister be able to quote rather authoritatively from biblical passages and apply them to the life of the parishioners in his sermon. In other words, interpretation of the Bible is simply not a cause for serious, protracted disagreement between the pulpit and the pew.

In some instances, where the educational level of the members is relatively high, it would be acceptable if the minister were a self-made, self-educated man, but even this would not be tolerated in too many places. There are a number of cases in which the minister has pastored a church for twenty years or more, and where the congregation has become more highly educated since World War II. The pastor might well have only a high-school diploma plus "some courses" at a local seminary. The younger peo ple of the church who grew up under his early pastorate are now college graduates in some cases, and they continue to attend the church. This does not present the problem voiced earlier by the A.M.E. bishops. For one thing, the pastor is usually in his late fifties or older, and he is looked upon by the younger, better educated members as a father figure, and as one who has special talents and a special relationship to the church, developed over decades. He probably baptized the younger members; he christened their children; he has taken the younger members into the governing bodies of the church: trustee board, deacon board. In the final analysis, his relationship to the church is such that it is far more comfortable for the better educated members to remain with "their" church and with "their" pastor than it would be for them to leave and find another church where they would, so to speak, have to start all over again in learning the church and the minister. It is also likely, however, that when the time comes to choose or call a new pastor, the congregation will probably require one who has more formal training than the previous pastor.

There is a noticeable trend, however, of those parishioners who achieve a higher education to leave the church of their youth—usually Baptist or Methodist—and to join one of the "high" churches: Presbyterian, Episcopalian, Catholic, Unitarian.

On balance, it would be accurate to say that in many places there is an inclination toward demanding a better-trained minister—both in terms of general formal education and a seminary background. Some churches are requiring their new pastor to display evidence both of the call and of preparation. There is, after all, some prestige to be derived from having a minister with college degrees after his name. And given the fact that there is—though many ministers and members would deny it—a fair amount of competition between the various churches in a community, a pastor with evidence of advanced formal training lends increased prestige to the church.

This will be noticed more in the cities, North and South, than in the rural areas. It is the cities where most blacks go who have obtained more formal education. In the rural areas and even in some small towns (perhaps less than three to five thousand in population), it is unlikely that a congregation will impose such requirements. In the first place, the general educational level of the congregation itself will probably not exceed a high-school diploma, and will more likely approach eighth grade. In addition, it is far more difficult to attract a young seminary-trained minister to such a place. He probably prefers a more urban setting, even if it means accepting a position as an assistant minister. A final important consideration is that the rural or small-town congregation might feel that the seminarian is "too educated" for their church. He might come and "talk over our heads." In essence, as stated in Chapter I, the pastor and pew seek their kind. They usually are not too different from each other, educationally. Both are aware that if the relationship is to be a protracted, comfortable one, there must be definite educational compatibility.

This matter is handled on a rather individual basis in most black churches. That is, it is essentially a matter between the individual congregation and the prospective minister. This, of course, is less often the case in more nationally structured church bodies such as the Methodist, Presbyterian, A.M.E., A.M.E. Zion, C.M.E. and certainly the Roman Catholic churches. One also finds a black ministry in these latter churches that has a greater amount of formal and theological training than the ministry in the Baptist and other independent black churches.

This is not to say that the Baptists have not taken an interest in the education of their ministers. In 1890, the black Baptists supported forty-six educational institutions, but training for the ministry was only part of the work. Out of 4,106 students, 181 were preparing to be ministers.[11] The schools were small, some of them at first meeting at night in the basement of various local Baptist churches. There were twelve schools owned and managed by the (white) American Baptist Home Mission Society for the education of black people. There were 2,692 students attending them in 1890, 340 of whom were preparing for the ministry.

Without question, from such meager beginnings substantial efforts were made, but not very much was accomplished in the more-than-half century since 1890. The question of education constantly came before the black Baptist ministers in their national sessions. In 1956, the president of the National Baptist Convention, U.S.A., Inc., Reverend Joseph H. Jackson, recommended a ten-year educational plan for the Convention. The plan called for a commission on education consisting of the presidents of the Baptist schools and teachers within the jurisdiction of the National Baptist Convention, and it would study the educational content of all the Baptist schools. Perhaps, it was suggested, a merger of some of the schools would take place, while the programs of others would be expanded. Reverend Jackson suggested that the National Baptist Convention launch an educational drive for ten million dollars, half of which was to be invested for endowments and the other half for expansion. He hoped that these goals would be achieved within ten years, and stated that the educational institutions "must be placed on a higher scholastic standard." [12]

These recommendations, several years later, remained largely unaccomplished. In 1964, an article in *Ebony* stated:

> The educational foundation is a Jackson-sponsored plan which seeks to build a $10-million fund for college scholarships, missionary education and capital improvements at Convention-supported seminaries and colleges. The Convention has already endowed a $10,000 scholarship fund at Roosevelt University in Chicago,* but plans are to expand the student-help program into one of the largest church-related programs in existence.[13]

* This is not a Convention-supported institution. It is a predominantly white university in downtown Chicago with a sizable black-student enrollment since its inception in 1945.

Bishops in the A.M.E. Church have, over the years, pronounced their interest in education of ministers of that church. At the General Conference in 1916 in Philadelphia, the following announcement was made:

> The class of 1908, consisting of Bishops H. B. Parks, J. S. Flipper, J. Albert Johnson, and W. H. Heard, after due consideration decided to offer a scholarship of two hundred dollars ($200) each year for four years in any first-class Methodist Theological Seminary in America or in a foreign country upon the following conditions:
>
> First, all applicants must be college graduates and licensed to preach in the African Methodist Episcopal Church, and shall have had at least one year's experience in our itinerancy.
>
> Second, all applicants must be sound in body, mind, and morals.
>
> Third, all applicants must pass a competitive examination before a competent committee at the place where the applicants reside unless otherwise ordered.[14]

It is accurate to state that the histories are full of statements of good intentions and plans to further education of the ministry. And from time to time there is evidence of individual and collective efforts and contributions. For the most part, however, educational endeavors on behalf of the black ministry have suffered from lack of adequate financial resources—from within and without. The schools founded by blacks and whites have remained relatively small and financially poor. This is still a serious problem in the 1970's, as indeed it was after the Civil War in the 1860's.

Black Preachers as Educators

Bishop Daniel Payne of the A.M.E. Church went off to England for one year in 1867 to raise money for Wilber-

force University. The school had been founded by the
A.M.E. Church in 1863 in Ohio, and it was the first college
owned and operated by blacks for blacks. Payne was the
first black president of a black college. During his relatively unsuccessful journey, he was told by one English
lady, "If you had come just after the war, when English
enthusiasm was at its height, you might have obtained
something, but now I fear it is too late." [15] He experienced
what black fund-raisers have experienced through the
years: There are times when "black causes" are timely and
fashionable, and that is the time to strike.

While black people themselves have contributed sums
to their educational institutions, these sums have remained small largely because the black contributors simply
have not had large resources to draw from. During the
period following the Civil War, there were reports that
blacks occasionally contributed. In 1880, the black population of Texas contributed nearly two thousand dollars
in ten months toward the establishment of Bishop Baptist
College in Marshall, Texas. In 1874, the black Baptist
Convention at Tuscaloosa, Alabama, through the efforts
of a Reverend W. H. Alpine, raised a thousand dollars
from black churches to support Selma University, a school
in Selma, Alabama, for black preachers. Black people later
paid for thirty-six acres and a building in 1878, at a cost
of three thousand dollars. Reverend McAlpine, born a
slave, was made president of the school in 1881.

Most of the money for black schools in the early years
following slavery—and for a substantial portion of the
teaching staffs—were supplied by Northern white philan-
thropists. Blacks were very instrumental in many places
in providing their church properties for classroom space,
as well as doing a lot of the brick-masonry and carpentry
work in constructing new buildings. Blacks had a greater
abundance of skills than money, and these they offered
liberally in many places. A Baptist school, Wayland Semi-

nary in Washington, D.C., was built in 1873–74, with much of the work done by blacks. Dr. A. W. Pegues has observed: "The walls from the foundation to the crowning were constructed by colored bricklayers under the supervision of a master-workman, an ex-slave from Virginia, who purchased his own freedom before the war." [16] Many of the initial buildings on black campuses were constructed by the black students. At Shaw University in Raleigh, North Carolina, "an industrial building was erected in 1887. President Tupper planned and superintended the erection of the buildings, even to the making of the brick on the premises. Much of the work was done by students." [17] In all instances, the black preachers and their churches were instrumental in these efforts.

Blacks in Florida raised two thousand dollars under the leadership of several Baptist preachers to aid in the establishment of the Florida Institute in 1873 in Live Oak, Florida.

This small town in Florida was also the place of an unfortunate attempt to establish a school for blacks. In 1866, the A.M.E. Church sent the Reverend Charles H. Pearce to the state to raise money, with a contract to keep 16 percent of all he collected for his time and expenses. The school was envisioned as an institution to prepare black men for the ministry. Reverend Pearce was vigorous in his appeals and received contributions ranging from money to mules. The Reverend Charles Summer Long, in a history of the A.M.E. Church in Florida, noted:

> In one of his speeches delivered in the City of Talla-
> hassee, so greatly did he picture the need of his school
> to his hearers, that General M. S. Littlefield, the rail-
> road magnate of Florida, came forward and gave twenty
> thousand dollars in State Script and railroad bonds.
> Hon. Simeon B. Conaver, treasurer of the State, gave
> a fine pair of mules and a wagon, Lieutenant-General

William H. Gleason gave 640 acres of land in Volusia County, Fla., and other men gave smaller amounts to the school.[18]

The school had a very rough beginning owing to the lack of funds, in spite of these initial contributions and the oratorical abilities of Reverend Pearce. It was chartered by the state legislature in 1872 and named Brown Theological Institute. These kinds of ventures could not escape the hustlers, those out to make money for themselves, and as a consequence some efforts were failures. Such was the case with Brown University (the name was changed in 1874). Reverend Long wrote:

> Bishop T. M. D. Ward, D.D., who succeeded Bishop John M. Brown in the Fla. Conference took charge of the school work according to the Charter, and appointed a white man, Dr. Sidney as traveling agent for the school; to collect money and superintend the work. He collected more than three thousand dollars from the people as his receipts showed. He failed to pay the carpenters; used the money for self aggrandisement and ran away; but for his dishonest deeds to the people who had just been made free, was over taken in a storm, and the great God of the Heavens strangled him to death beneath the maddening waters of the Atlantic, to await the judgement trumpet of the Arch Angel. The people became disheartened and refused to give any more money toward the building; the carpenters sued the board of trustees and obtained a judgement in the court; the building was sold to the highest bidder, the timber and other material was disposed of, and thus ended Brown Theological Institute and Brown University.[19]

In addition to this instance of outright fraud and larceny, there were occasions when ministers would accuse each other of not approaching the matter of fund-raising

in the most efficient manner. Notwithstanding Bishop
Payne's account of his lack of success in England, one
A.M.E. bishop, Charles Spencer Smith, felt that Payne's
problems were as much a cause of his personal failures as
they were a lack of enthusiasm on the part of Englishmen.
In his history of the Church, he wrote:

> Despite the author's veneration for Bishop Payne, he
> is led to observe that he views the cause of the Bishop's
> financial failure from a different angle from what he
> did. The strain of aristocracy in his blood insisted on
> his seeking social favors and amenities, and the asso-
> ciation of the nobility and the cultured, rather than
> going around with an open hand in the attitude of a
> beggar.[20]

In the sixty years after the Civil War, black denominations and churches had established approximately forty
institutions that would be considered full-fledged colleges
and universities. Many of these had a very strong theological orientation, because their primary purpose was to train
students for the ministry, or at least to inculcate a strong
sense of Christian values in their students. There were
many other schools, of course, on the elementary and
secondary levels that were aided by black churches. Professor E. Franklin Frazier has noted:

> The work of the Negro preacher in establishing schools
> was especially important since the southern States pro-
> vided only a pittance of public funds for the education
> of Negro children. When the Julius Rosenwald Fund
> contributed to the building of more than 5,000 schools
> for Negroes in the South in order to stimulate the pub-
> lic authorities to appropriate money for Negro schools,
> Negro churches played an important role in making
> possible the schools aided by the Rosenwald Fund.
> Negroes contributed 17 per cent of the total cost of the

schools which amounted to over $28,000,000. They raised most of their share in this amount through church suppers and programmes under the auspices of their churches.[21]

It is also clear that the church leaders have exercised considerable authority on the boards of trustees of many of the colleges. The college presidents, in many cases, owe their jobs and a substantial portion of their budgets to the bishops and preachers, and it would not be wise for the presidents to clash with them too often. Occasionally, rivalry among bishops over the management of a school has reached the press. For the most part, these incidents are publicly denied by the participants, but privately, professors and administrators on some of the campuses affirm their validity. One professor at an A.M.E. Zion school stated: "No doubt about it. Power lies with those bishops, and the Administration dances to their tune." Another stated: "If ever there's a fight between the bishops on the board—and don't let anybody tell you that that doesn't happen—the worst thing that can happen is to get caught in the middle. Those people pay our salaries. We try to stay out of it."

One rumored incident over the selection of the president of Livingstone College in Salisbury, North Carolina, was reported in *The Pittsburgh Courier* (a widely read weekly black newspaper) in 1958. The initial article read:

> It was rumored on the campus that a bitter undercover fight had developed within the board of trustees over the election group. One faction was led by Bishop W. J. Walls, senior Bishop of the A.M.E. Zion Church and chairman of the board of trustees, who favored Prof. J. H. Brockett, the acting president, and another group favored Dr. Samuel E. Duncan, led by Bishop C. Ewbank Tucker of the 10th Episcopal District.

Bishop Walls strongly denied this rumor and wrote a letter to the *Courier:*

> If the friends of Bishop Tucker or himself seek prominence for him politically, they had better drive their teams to a better market rather than play Livingstone College into disastrous personal politics.
>
> Those who work hardest for the school and who have done most for it, disdain the man or persons who seek to misrepresent us as cheapening the great cause of Christian education by dragging Livingstone College, or the cause of human uplift and education into ward-heeling politics.
>
> Unfortunately, some feel they need this kind of bogus publicity. . . .
>
> It would seem that your paper would sift such an article for its source and truth before it is published.[22]

It would not be surprising if such struggles did, in fact, occur on the boards. One can expect black-owned, church-related colleges to be no different from other schools in this regard. It would indeed be rather unusual if a group of men who felt intensely about a matter as important as school governance did not occasionally clash over policies and appointments. To believe otherwise is to assume that the bishops are angels and not men—a proposition even they will probably deny.

From time to time, the church bodies have examined their educational institutions and recommended major changes in overall trustee management. In 1958, a commission on educational institutions of the A.M.E. Church made such an analysis. The Church supervised nine schools, four of which at that time were accredited by the Southern Association of Colleges and Secondary Schools. In 1957, the A.M.E. Church gave $900,000 to the nine schools, and there was a total student body of three thousand, 1,179 of whom belonged to the A.M.E. Church.

The commission criticized the "unwieldy"-sized trustee boards. One college in Jacksonville, Florida, Edward Waters College, had a five-hundred-member board. It was suggested that such boards should not exceed twenty-one members. Because of past disputes between college presidents and the presiding bishop, the commission recommended that residences for church bishops on the campuses be removed "to avoid interference." Another practice severely condemned involved the awarding of numerous honorary degrees in one year, many of them to clergy. Daniel Payne College gave twenty-four such degrees in 1957.

Some black preachers have almost been as actively interested in the church schools as they have in their individual churches. The preacher is looked upon as a major money-raiser in the black community, and his efforts on behalf of a college can be crucial to the budget of that school. Using a mixture of religious appeals and oratorical skills, the minister can coax, cajole, beg and plead with his congregation to dig just a little bit deeper—for one more passing of the collection plate. His church is the base for sustained drives for funds, as opposed to a one-shot appeal. And most important is the minister's ability, often invoked, to play on the competitive spirit of his parishioners. He reminds them that their church should not be announced as being behind any other church in its contributions, because "we all know, like God, First Baptist [or whatever name] is generous and we know it is more blessed to give than to receive." Occasionally pulpits are made available to speakers and choirs from various colleges who make appeals for funds during a special program. At times an alumnus or alumna of the college will be a member of the church, and with the minister's backing will conduct a sustained drive—coordinated, always, with the other fund drives being conducted in the church—

for contributions to the college. If the minister is particularly successful in raising money for the school, he can expect an invitation from the college to speak and even, possibly, a position on the board of trustees or an honorary degree. The many "Reverend Doctors" in the pulpits of black churches are not, in most cases, holders of earned academic degrees.

Thus, as the church and the minister have been mainstays in the black community generally, they have also been crucial from the beginning in black education—at all levels. In the 1970's, in spite of the increased earning power of many black parishioners, the church cannot provide anything like the amount of money needed to support the budgets of the various black colleges and universities. This has always been the case. But many ministers, through their churches, are active supporters of the United Negro College Fund. They make appeals on behalf of the Fund; they display Fund posters in their vestibules, and they run announcements of UNCF drives in their church papers.

Most of the larger churches have scholarship programs of varying sizes for youngsters in the congregation. And most of these scholarships are not limited only to those students preparing for a career in the ministry. In fact, no such limitation is known to exist today. Where there is no organized, continuing program, it is not unknown for a minister on a given Sunday morning to make a special appeal for a collection to support the son or daughter of a member going or preparing to go to college. With the greater availability of scholarship sources from the government and private foundations, this kind of appeal is not done as much as it was, say, before World War II, when scholarships were fewer. But one minister in 1970 stated: "If I see a youngster trying to better him or herself, and I know the family's doing all it can, I won't hesitate a minute to ask the people in the church to help out. And

I'll be the first to go in my pocket. You ask any of them. They'll tell you." Because it is such a relatively small sum and can reach only a very few students, most ministers indicate they would prefer giving to an organized scholarship program. But the individualized approach has been and is being used.

Neither are the ministers unaware of the advantages and disadvantages of such activity. One minister in Harlem recalled, "I had a mother come to see me and ask if I would help her boy the way I helped so-and-so's child. You know. Well, you got to be careful. You see."

On the other hand, there is a certain amount of benefit to be derived from this kind of "patronage." It helps to build loyalty and support in much the same way that patronage functions in political parties. Although most ministers would probably, and perhaps sincerely, deny that this is even the slightest motivation, it is also true that some will state privately, if not publicly, that patronage has these definite benefits for the church—and for his pastorate. These preachers are, in many instances, shrewd organizers who understand what is required, at times, to build and maintain thriving organizations. They are, in other words, quite frequently master politicians. They know that caring for their congregation (constituents)— and helping a family finance a child's education is one way of providing immediate tangible support—often means protecting their positions in the pulpit.

This proposition was mentioned to one minister whose church had paid the tuition for a member's child, and it was established that this was not a new practice in the church. When asked if he felt this had "political" benefits for the church, the minister responded: "Well, son, I'm a preacher, not a politician. I don't mix in politics. I just try to help people, like the Lord says do."

Fair enough!

V

Preachers and
Political Action

The base of American electoral politics is the local community. Those politicians who have achieved positions of national political power have done so normally as a result of having a strong base of support in their local communities, counties and, sometimes, states. It is at the local level that the black preacher has exerted the greatest political influence. Some have, of course, achieved national office in the Congress: three (Richard Harvey Cain from South Carolina; Jeremiah Haralson from Alabama; Hiram Rhodes Revels, senator from Mississippi) were members of the Congress during Reconstruction; Reverend Adam Clayton Powell, Jr., served more than twenty-two years and became chairman of the powerful House Committee on Labor and Education; and the first congressman from Washington, D.C., Walter E. Fauntroy, is a minister.

Generally, black preachers have been politically active at the local community levels, either as office holders, leaders of pressure groups, influential members of political parties or simply as leaders of their individual churches. In some cases, it has been rather easy for them to accept political roles if they have wanted them. Because ministers are leaders of organized bodies, other politicians see them as assets in reaching people. In addition, they have known that one way to serve their parishioners is to be able to deliver goods and services obtainable from the political system.

The general pattern has been to enter the ministry, build up a sizable church and personal following and then combine parish work with political work. Very seldom will the preacher give up his church when he enters politics. In a sense that would be tantamount to giving up one's political home base, which simply is not done. It is from the base of the church that the minister gets appointed to various local governmental boards and commissions. It is the church base that serves as his leverage if he decides to move into local political-party councils. If he is able to obtain the endorsement of a local ministerial association, so much the better.

One of the best modern examples of a preacher-politician using his church as his primary base of political operation and building upon that base a powerful political career, is of course, the Reverend Adam Clayton Powell, Jr. When he took over the pastorate of Abyssinian Baptist Church in Harlem in 1937, following the retirement of his father, he assumed the leadership of one of the oldest and largest black churches in the world. The church had a membership of around 11,000, a staff of thirty-three and property valued close to a half-million dollars. In 1933, its annual budget was $46,000. The church held three or four services on Sunday to accommodate the worshipers, and it published a community newspaper with a circulation of 55,000.

From 1931 Powell had served as business manager and director of the social and educational programs of the church. He also had a column in the weekly black newspaper. For a number of years throughout the 1930's, he had been active in protest movements and demonstrations in Harlem against unfair employment practices, poor housing, poor medical facilities and a number of other issues. Thus he had already established a high degree of visibility and had achieved a reputation for being outspoken and "radical" when he became the leader of the church.

Using the church as his base, he was elected to the city council and from there to a seat in the House of Representatives in 1944. Because of the fragmented nature of New York City politics, especially in the early 1950's, Powell could maintain his Abyssinian base pretty much independently of the city machine. In elections he did not have to rely on city party workers who owed their allegiance to a downtown machine, but rather he could recruit hundreds, if not thousands, of volunteer church workers. The church became, then, a kind of political-party club in its own right. It did what many political machines did: It took care of some of the daily economic needs of those who belonged to the church and came for help. It had, in other words, its own patronage system, and Powell, as the master politician, could rely on that base to sustain him through many national and local political struggles. Some of his Sunday-morning sermons were clearly political speeches, and no attempt was made on his part to make them seem or be otherwise. From this base he rose to be one of the most powerful politicians, black or white, in the country, a position he maintained until the mid-1960's.

The Powell–Abyssinian Baptist Church alliance and result could not be duplicated exactly in other parts of the country, but there are many instances in which black preachers have relied heavily on their church as a springboard into politics. This is a phenomenon that dates back to Reconstruction after the Civil War, if not before that time.

Political Activists During Reconstruction

After the Civil War, black preachers played an important role in politics. Their leadership in this field was not as exclusive as it was in education in relation to other black professions, but it was nonetheless substantially felt. Whereas most black schools were started and led either by Northern whites or Southern black ministers, in politics there were more black lawyers and artisans who were active. For example, of the twenty-two blacks in the Congress from 1870 to 1901, six were lawyers, three were preachers, four were farmers, two were public officials and the seven remaining were artisans of several trades: barber, bricklayer, tailor.

The preachers, however, relying on the local church base, were quite active in the state constitutional conventions and in local and state offices. The Reverend J. T. White, a Baptist preacher in Arkansas, was active in the Constitutional Convention and the legislature of that state for several terms. All the time, he built and pastored churches in Helena and Little Rock. The Reverend Jesse Freeman Boulden was one of the first black "kingmakers" in American politics. Operating out of Mississippi, he helped manage the successful campaigns of the two black candidates to the United States Senate, Hiram R. Revels and Blanche K. Bruce. He also served for a while as a member of the Mississippi legislature, after participating in the Mississippi Republican State Convention in 1867.

In 1869, a black Methodist minister, James Lynch, was elected Secretary of State in Mississippi on the Republican ticket. A year earlier, at the Mississippi Constitutional Convention, to which Lynch was selected as a delegate, a white delegate moved that the word "colored" be listed on the rolls beside the name of each black delegate. Reverend Lynch immediately moved that the rolls also reflect the color of each delegate's hair. This kind of sensitivity to any possible act of racial discrimination characterized the attitude and action of a number of politically involved preachers of that time.

The first black member of the West Virginia legislature, elected in 1896, was Reverend Christopher H. Payne. His career, like that of a number of other black preachers during that time, included several professions: teacher, lawyer, preacher, politician, editor.

General political and civil rights of black people concerned many ministers during this period. The General Conference of the A.M.E. Church, meeting in Nashville in 1872, passed several resolutions on the subject. Segregation, discrimination and racial bigotry were rampant in the country, and black travelers were the victims of many acts of racial hatred and harassment. One series of resolutions read:

> Whereas, certain railroad companies in the States of Georgia, Tennessee, and Kentucky have assumed to make regulations violative of the said constitutional amendment by making the colored people who travel on their roads pay first-class fare, and thrusting them into second-class cars because of their color, and often abusing our wives and children by ejecting them from first-class cars; therefore, . . .
>
> Resolved, that we, the representatives of the largest body of Christians of the African race in this country, hereby enter our solemn protest against this relic of barbarism and American slavery, as inconsistent with the rights of man and the principles which underlie our enlightened government.
>
> Resolved, that we enter our protest against the treatment and insults offered to the bishops and delegates of this General Conference on these roads while coming to Nashville.

Resolved, that we hereby pray the Congress of the United States, now in session, to pass the "Civil Rights Bill," now pending, and offered by the Hon. Charles Sumner, of Massachustts, to the end that equal rights may be awarded to every American citizen traveling on the highways of the nation.[1]

Occasionally, records reveal the awareness of some ministers of the political implications of their acts. And at times, as in 1876, these are noted with some irony and cynical humor. In that year a group of A.M.E. bishops, meeting in Washington, D.C., were invited to have lunch with James G. Blaine. This act of social interaction, had it been generally known, would have been enough to bring strong criticism from some circles. At that time blacks and whites, in most places (and certainly not in the South), simply did not eat together. That was an act of social equality not authorized by the Thirteenth and Fourteenth Amendments. It was somewhat permissible to have meetings together, but not to have "eatin' meetin's." Present at the lunch was the future President of the United States, James A. Garfield. Bishop Daniel Payne wrote that wine was served and the luncheon talk was witty and humorous. ("From the wine the bishops nobly abstained, but fully enjoyed the sparkling wit and risible humor. Mr. Garfield seemed as joyful as any other of the guests." [2]) Bishop Charles S. Smith, commenting later that no one foresaw then that in a few years Garfield would become President, also made note of the potential political damage the Democrats would have tried to inflict on him by publicizing the luncheon:

By the way, what a furore it would have created had it been noised abroad! With what pitilessness, mercilessness, and spleen would a certain political party have made it the vehicle by which to hurl against Mr. Garfield the dogma of "social equality!" [3]

With the end of Reconstruction, the political activity of most black preachers, like that of most blacks, generally, came to an end. Many returned full-time to the pulpit and to ministering to their parishioners on the daily individual basis with which they were most familiar. Some, as noted in Chapter IV, turned more to educational endeavors. For the last quarter of the nineteenth century, politics for black Americans was at a low point in both the North and the South. The national atmosphere was not conducive to black people's playing an active political role. A few black ministers, along with a handful of other black spokesmen, continued to speak out and to encourage black political action and to protest against racial injustice. But they did not have a national platform and there was not even slight receptivity in the government to appeals for alleviation of racial problems.

Professor E. Franklin Frazier has noted that "As the result of the elimination of Negroes from the political life of the American community, the Negro church became the arena of their political activities." [4] During this period the Baptists formed, split and re-formed. Many new black churches were organized (see Chapter III). Politics within the church, with the preachers at the helm, accelerated. In the church, black people could get elected to offices that had prestige and institutional power, when they could not aspire to public offices. A young black boy might not dream of someday becoming President of the United States, but he could always dream of becoming a bishop in the A.M.E. or A.M.E. Zion churches or a highly respected minister of First Baptist or Tabernacle.

Church splits were prevalent during this period. In many ways, the black community in the United States was forced to turn in upon itself and to create parallel institutions of self-maintenance and self-development. Ministers were crucial in this process of cultural transformation and adaptation, and the organizational skills so necessary in the public arena were no less necessary in the church arena. In fact, it is accurate to say that many blacks learned about organizations, acquired political skills and developed an ability to work with and lead people through the institution of the church.

There is a widespread notion that the black community is a vast wasteland of social disorganization. In some respects, this view has validity in terms of economic matters. But, especially in the South during the latter part of the nineteenth century and the turn of the twentieth century, there were highly elaborate religious structures within the churches which provided more than a fair amount of social organization and stability in the black community. This fact has been overlooked by many social scientists in their analyses of the black family and the black community. Many churches, more in the small towns and urban centers than in the rural sectors, had and have a half dozen or more organized committees and boards, each with its own chairman, vice-chairman, officers and members. These groups meet, conduct business, raise money and make reports. They develop annual programs, devise budgets and operate toward certain predetermined goals: raising a certain amount of money for the new Sunday-school building; implementing a scholarship program; putting on a talent or fashion show; planning a picnic outing for the church. Sitting on top of this is the black preacher, coordinating, supervising, advising, adjudicating—in some instances, serving as a political broker.

These church structures began to take shape on a large scale after Reconstruction. The preachers and the people had the time and inclination to devote to them, and church memberships grew rapidly during this period. What the black people could not realize in the public political arena, they sought to achieve in their own intracommunity institutions, primarily the church.

As National Spokesmen

Although the preachers have been most effective in their local churches and local communities, they have continued to make pronouncements on national issues. These statements are usually made before national bodies, and the appeal has largely been moralistic in nature. That is, at times, the preachers have stated that they "represent" millions of black people, with the veiled hint that these constituents represent votes. But for the most part, they have not really strongly suggested that they can deliver a bloc of nationally mobilized black votes. This claim has been left to secular leaders in the civil-rights organizations to make, and the ministers have confined themselves to going on record against the immorality of certain racial practices. In some cases, specific programs of political action have been proposed for churches to pursue, but generally the national body has not assumed the responsibility for implementing such programs. A notable exception is the statement issued in June, 1971, by the Interreligious Foundation for Community Organization, Inc. (IFCO), on apartheid in South Africa (discussed below).

After World War I, the country experienced a number of violent riots against and lynchings of blacks. The perpetrators of these acts went unpunished by local law-enforcement agencies, but the A.M.E. General Conference of 1920 issued a statement condemning this situation:

> The African Methodist Episcopal Church equally marshalls every fiber of its Christian manhood, and all its moral and intellectual strength against the burning,

mutilating, or lynching of any human being of any race
by mob violence. . . .

We protest in the name of God and the laudable
principles of justice against any and every act of mob
violence as a punishment for crime; and we appeal to
the Christian conscience of this country to rise to the
exalted plane of liberty, justice, right, and the elements
that constitute stable and established government, and
to protect every citizen, regardless of race, color, or
previous condition of servitude, in every right, privilege, and immunity guaranteed by the Constitution of
the United States of America and the States thereof.[5]

The bishops of the Church stated that they were for "law
and order" and wanted to see all criminals prosecuted.
The use of this phrase in the 1920's by blacks stand in
ironic contrast to groups and individuals using it in the
1970's. Today it is understood as a code phrase against
black rioting. Fifty years ago, it was used specifically to
call for the protection of blacks against white lynch mobs.

The A.M.E. ministers and bishops also supported the
Dyer Anti-Lynching Bill in the Congress of 1922. The bill
passed the House of Representatives several times, but was
killed by the filibuster in the Senate each time.

In the 1950's, the National Baptist Convention, U.S.A.,
Inc., the largest black denomination, made several pronouncements in favor of the rights of blacks and for general recognition in the body politic. At times, there is an
indication of political naïveté as evidenced by the following comment:

. . . in 1955 the Convention petitioned Congress on
behalf of its members to make May 17, the day of the
Supreme Court's historic decision on public schools, a
legal holiday. On January 25, a bill was promptly introduced as a result of this petition. Bill H.R. 3016 would
have established the holiday. It did not pass, but its

prompt introduction and consideration reflect the Convention's prestige and growing importance as a principal spokesman for the aspirations of the American Negro.[6]

There was no indication that a nationwide drive was conducted by the ministers to pressure the Congress to pass the bill. The fact that the proposed legislation was introduced should not be considered a measure of the organization's political power, inasmuch as the *introduction* of a bill was not a particularly difficult feat to achieve in the Congress, and the records do not indicate that serious "consideration" was given to the bill.

The Baptist Convention did, however, take stands against violent treatment of blacks in the South—of which there was a great deal. In a telegram to the governor of Mississippi, the organization officially protested the harassment of a black minister, the Reverend H. Dupree, by a group of whites. Reverend Dupree pastored four rural churches in Mississippi, and he had been an active civic leader in that state for several years. He and his family were threatened and driven from their home in the middle of the night by a mob. He appeared (in a borrowed suit) before the National Baptist Convention in San Francisco and told his story. He had been left destitute, and his son, who was preparing to enter college, was now financially unable to go. The governor of Mississippi, of course, did not respond to the telegram sent by the Convention's president, Reverend Joseph H. Jackson. But the group responded in a way that it was most adept at, that is, by providing immediate relief for the minister. A collection was taken and turned over to Reverend Dupree, and he was given a job by the Convention for six months. His son's immediate college expenses were met. The black church is noted in the black community as the one local institution capable of providing relief on the spot with a minimum of red tape. And this has been no small part of its power and influence among its followers.

With the advent of the mid-1960's and the appearance of "Black Power," summer rioting in the black urban areas and the acceleration of the war in Vietnam, black preachers became more vocal in their pronouncements—sometimes conflicting with one another. In 1966, the cry of "Black Power," led by Stokely Carmichael and the Student Nonviolent Coordinating Committee (SNCC), was sweeping the country. Public and private figures, secular and sectarian groups and individuals lined up for or against the ideology. Some saw it as a new hope for oppressed blacks; others interpreted it as a negative phenomenon serving only to polarize further whites and blacks in the country. It was a dynamic, dramatic occurrence on the civil-rights scene, and few people at all concerned about racial problems in the country could remain neutral on the subject.

Dr. Martin Luther King, Jr., the most prominent and influential black religious leader in the country, had serious reservations about the term. He was involved with Stokely Carmichael and Floyd McKissick of CORE in a mass march in Mississippi in June, 1966, when the term was introduced into the language of the modern civil-rights struggle. King preferred to use words such as "black consciousness" or "black equality." He felt they were less violence-laden. He wrote:

> Immediately, I had reservations about its use. I had the deep feeling that it was an unfortunate choice of words for a slogan. Moreover, I saw it bringing about division within the ranks of the marchers. For a day or two there was fierce competition between those who were wedded to the Black Power slogan and those wedded to Freedom Now. Speakers on each side sought

desperately to get the crowds to chant their slogan the loudest.

Sensing this widening split in our ranks, I asked Stokely and Floyd to join me in a frank discussion of the problem. We met the next morning, along with members of each of our staffs, in a small Catholic parish house in Yazoo City. For five long hours I pleaded with the group to abandon the Black Power slogan. It was my contention that a leader has to be concerned about the problem of semantics. Each word, I said, has a denotative meaning—its explicit and recognized sense—and a connotative meaning—its suggestive sense. While the concept of legitimate Black Power might be denotatively sound, the slogan "Black Power" carried the wrong connotations. I mentioned the implications of violence that the press had already attached to the phrase. And I went on to say that some of the rash statements on the part of a few marchers only reinforced this impression.[7]

The debate was not terminated with that meeting, nor were the differences reconciled.

The following month, July, 1966, a group of thirty-two black ministers met at the Bethel African Methodist Episcopal Church in Philadelphia, the church founded by Reverend Richard Allen. Led by a black minister, Benjamin F. Payton, the group issued a statement, saying in part, "We identify ourselves with the feelings and needs of the dispossessed of our nation, from whom most of the cry for Black Power comes. It is a legitimate cry."

A few weeks later the group, soon to call itself the National Committee of Black Churchmen (NCBC), met at the Mother African Methodist Episcopal Zion Church in New York. This church was founded by Reverend James Varick, who, in 1822, became the first bishop of the A.M.E. Zion Church. On July 31, 1966, the NCBC placed a full-page advertisement in *The New York Times*. Whereas earlier pronouncements of black clergy had appealed largely to the goodwill and conscience of the society, the new group of black preachers distinctly pointed out the meaninglessness of such an appeal:

> We, an informal group of Negro churchmen in America, are deeply disturbed about the crisis brought upon our country by historic distortions of important human realities in the controversy about "black power." What we see shining through the variety of rhetoric is not anything new but the same old problem of power and race which has faced our beloved country since 1619. . . . The fundamental distortion facing us in this controversy about Black Power is rooted in a gross imbalance of power and conscience between Negroes and white Americans. . . . The power of white men is corrupted because it meets little meaningful resistance from Negroes to temper it and keep white men from aping God. The conscience of black men is corrupted because, not having power to implement the demands of conscience, the concern for justice is transmuted into a distorted form of love, which in the absence of justice, becomes chaotic self-surrender. Powerlessness breeds a race of beggars. We are faced with a situation where powerless conscience meets conscienceless power, threatening the very foundations of our Nation.

Reverend Leon W. Watts II, one of the founders and officers of NCBC, summed up the position of the group:

> This group of ecclesiastical renegades, denominational radicals and *mad* preachers, pushed by the wave of growing Black militancy and the unresponsiveness of the white denominations to the Black condition, continued to meet. We found ourselves regarded as the true "outsiders": neither fish nor fowl; not really the enemy, but not really the recognized ally to the Black community. Standing between us and the Black community was "white Christianity," which we allegedly

represented. That impression needed to be corrected posthaste.[8]

Another incident which created considerable controversy in the country and among clergy, black and white, was the demand, led by James Forman, that white churches pay reparations to black Americans for centuries of oppression. "We are . . . demanding of the white Christian churches and Jewish synagogues, that are part and parcel of the system of capitalism, that they begin to pay reparations to black people in this country. We are demanding $500,000,000 from the Christian white churches and the Jewish synagogues."

On May 4, 1969, Forman interrupted services at the large and prestigious Riverside Church in New York and presented the demands. Other confrontations occurred around the country in subsequent weeks. Three days after the Riverside confrontation, the board of trustees of NCBC supported the "principle of reparations," saying: "The white churches and synagogues undeniably have been the moral cement of the structure of racism in this nation. . . . . They are capable, out of their enormous corporate assets [of making] some reparation for their complicity in the exploitation of Blacks."

This incident found black preachers throughout the country once again lined up on both sides—for and against. But the fact that some black ministers would publicly and vigorously support such a movement indicated the distance many had come in their relationship to the black struggle. Clearly, a new black-conscious, black-power-oriented clergy was developing around the country. This has led some black ministers to begin to rethink their entire understanding of Christianity and to start articulating a "Black Theology," which will be discussed later in this chapter.

The war in Vietnam has also received attention from

the black clergy. Another national group, the Progressive National Baptist Convention, following the lead of Dr. Martin Luther King, Jr., and Reverend Ralph Abernathy, went on record in September, 1967, calling on President Lyndon B. Johnson "to turn the Vietnam conflict over to the UN and to withdraw troops from Vietnam immediately." Reverend Abernathy said, "It makes no sense at all to spend $5 million to kill one Vietcong soldier and declare ourselves unable to spend $50 to train a black man for responsible living at home."

King was severely criticized at the time by some secular and sectarian leaders for combining civil rights with foreign policy. But he relied on his philosophy of nonviolence to defend his stand. He answered: "It would be very inconsistent for me to teach and preach nonviolence in this situation and then applaud violence when thousands and thousands of people, both adults and children, are being maimed and mutilated and many killed in this war, so that I still feel and live by the principle, 'Thou shalt not kill.'"

Other black clergymen have decided to speak out on other foreign issues, particularly on South Africa. In June, 1971, the Interreligious Foundation for Community Organization (IFCO), issued a strong and clear statement calling for support of freedom-fighter groups in Angola, Zimbabwe, Mozambique and South Africa. This was the first time such a position had been taken by a national organization of black people. Leaders of IFCO had been invited to participate in a symposium to be held in Johannesburg, South Africa, under the auspices of the United States-South African Leadership Exchange Program. They rejected the invitation. "The divisions that have been created between Africans on both sides of the Atlantic Ocean must be healed. In its place must be developed understanding and unity of purpose. That purpose must not be tricky dialogue but complete liberation of African people throughout the world." Among other things, the organization called for churches to "contribute medicines, clothes, food and money directly to the African liberation organization," and "A specific form of assistance might be subsidy for the wives and children of the freedom fighters while they are on the front."

As Local Leaders

Most national black spokesmen and leaders must rely on the mass media to maintain their positions of leadership. They must appear or be featured with some degree of frequency in the news. The reason for this is obvious. Except for a very few organizations such as the NAACP, the Black Muslims, the Urban League, the Black Congressional Caucus and CORE, there are no black organizations with a national mass base, that is, organizations specially designed to deal with political issues.

Mass, public visibility is most important to national black spokesmen. They need not be elected by a popular vote cast by a prescribed, identifiable constituency; they need only be selected by those (essentially white) capable of giving them wide, public exposure.

The same *might* apply to leaders and spokesmen at the local, community level, but it need not, and with black preachers usually does not. A black preacher can be a legitimate leader and spokesman by relying on the pulpit, not the press. His support mechanisms are not dependent upon the mass media, but upon the church membership. He need not necessarily be influential with powerful white decision-makers, but with powerful black deacons in his church. The latter group may influence the former, but his base of support stems basically from the church. This means, of course, that he might not be known widely beyond his church and beyond a few decision-making circles in the town, but he is an influential local leader nonetheless.

There are at least three discernible types of preacher roles of political activism at the local level.

One type is the church-based local activist. He is influential in the community, town or city by virtue of his being the leader of a rather large church. He is invited to serve on community boards such as the community-action agency of an antipoverty program and the Model Cities board. He may receive an appointment to a city commission. He is frequently consulted by the public and private decision-makers—in City Hall, the chamber of commerce. It is not unusual for him to be a member of the board of directors of the local NAACP or Urban League. Politics, for him, is not at all a full-time or continuous activity. In fact, he might even deny that he is "politically active," because he will mean by that that he does not run for office or endorse candidates. He may describe himself as "simply a preacher, not a politician." But in a broader sense of the term, he is a political activist. His actions are simply not as visible or overt as those of some other activists. His base is his church. He has one office, and that is in the church. He will probably not be found in the inner circles of local political-party councils or at political rallies. But he may lend his name and support to a particular civil-rights cause. He will do this because he will see this not as "politics," but as "human rights," which is "above politics." If he is engaged in a private discussion of his role in the political community, he may easily say that he knows "how to get things done," meaning by this that he "has contacts." Again, this is not viewed as "political" in the traditional sense, because he views "politics" as basically a "dirty business," where people have to make compromises and deals.

The church-based local activist is highly inclined toward

individual action in civic affairs. He much prefers to make a telephone call to the mayor rather than to participate in a mass march on City Hall. This gives him the reputation with white decision-makers of being "respectable and responsible," and not a "rabble-rouser, radical or militant." Because his primary source of influence is his church, if he left the ministry, it is doubtful that he could carry his prestige and what power or influence he does have with him. He enjoys the respect of the community and church members who, in fact, see his service on community boards and city commissions as very laudable and beneficial to the church. The church, as a result of the pastor's participation, might be involved in a Head Start program or in a community health center sponsored by the Office of Economic Opportunity (O.E.O.). It might get special consideration from the urban-renewal authority in relocating displaced black residents. With some black churches, it is no small consideration to have a low-income housing complex for the elderly located nearby. Or for that matter, to have any sort of new housing development built in the vicinity of the church. These sorts of considerations are never discussed publicly from the pulpit and pew, but neither do they have to be. Black preachers and parishioners understand these things about politics and the consequences for the development and maintenance of their churches.

One black preacher who serves on a city planning board stated:

> Some people don't realize I have my ear to the ground. I know where my church is and I know where they're thinking of putting up that housing project and that shopping center where our folks will go. And when the folks downtown start talking about running a super highway through, you know, I'm right there with my pencil to help 'em draw some of those lines

and curves. And that's what we got to learn. How those people operate.

A second type of politically involved minister is the community-based local activist. He takes an active part in local electoral politics as well as in mass-oriented pressure-group politics. He may run for public office and serve as the leader of a political-action group. His church is his initial platform; it is where he got his start as a community-oriented person, but he probably does not combine the church structure with his political organization. In other words, his church office is physically separated from his political headquarters. This type of preacher will undoubtedly try to enlist the aid and support of the local ministerial association, and he will constantly urge it to take political stands. He is more prone to be "militant" than the church-based type, and he is less likely to shy away from mass, overt confrontation politics.

If his local activity becomes very successful or visible, he may gain national prominence, but it is always understood that his base of support and operation is the particular community from which he comes. One prime example is the Reverend Jesse Jackson of Chicago. While he is the national director of a new organization, Operation PUSH (People United to Save Humanity), his major strength is centered in Chicago. He has launched a number of protest campaigns in that city against discriminatory employment practices and has met with varying degrees of success. His close association with Dr. Martin Luther King, Jr., (he was with King in the Memphis motel when King was assassinated) prior to 1968 gave him added national exposure, and now he frequently makes speeches throughout the country and is generally recognized as a national spokesman. His church base is in Chicago, however, and it is that city in which he can mobilize the greatest political power to affect decision-making on a continuing basis. His structure is there; in all other places, he is invited in by other local leadership groups for temporary appearances. His new organization, formed in late 1971, has not established a network of local chapters around the country. One segment, PUSH-East, was started in New York in March, 1972. It is in Chicago that he would aspire to political office if he so decided. (In 1971, he challenged the Illinois state election laws in the courts. He did this before running in the mayoralty race in Chicago.)

His church services are held on Saturday mornings, and they are distinct combinations of religious worship and political rally. Many national and local political figures attend and appear in the pulpit. There is every indication, however, that Reverend Jackson will attempt to form a nationally effective organization commensurate with his growing personal national prestige and influence.

This type of black preacher is beginning to appear more and more in the South also. For many years black preachers were active in voters' leagues and in the local NAACP chapters, and after the late 1960's (and the passage of the Voting Rights Act of 1965) several started running for public office. In 1970, in Greene County, Alabama, an all-black slate on the National Democratic Party of Alabama ticket won every major local office. The powerful position of probate judge was won by a black preacher, William M. Branch, who pastored two rural Baptist churches. Another black Baptist preacher, Thomas E. Gilmore, was elected sheriff of the county. Both men had been politically active in the county for a number of years. Reverend Branch founded the local NAACP chapter, and Reverend Gilmore was a member of SNCC.

A third type of preacher activist is the man who uses his church as a specific base to launch and conduct civic programs of various sorts. He could be called the church-based programmatic activist. Unlike the first type, he is much more public and mass-oriented in his actions. Unlike the second type, he might well combine his church organization with the specific program of action. This minister also has a long history of antecedents in the black community. The black church, under the leadership of the minister, was the initial impetus of the establishment of many benevolent societies and mutual-aid societies long before the twentieth century.[9] These were some of the first efforts at self-development among black people in this country. The Free African Society, established in 1787 by the Reverends Richard Allen and Absalom Jones, was the first of the black mutual-aid societies. In the following decades, a number of such groups developed to aid their members during sickness, to provide for burial expenses and so forth. Most of these groups were church-related, and they gave birth later to some black insurance companies.

While this type of activity would not be considered "political action" in the traditionally understood sense of that term, it was activity clearly related to a particular sociopolitical economic environment. That is, most blacks were destitute and needed help. Their conditions were the result of a generally hostile larger society, and they needed to band together for survival and self-development. Thus, these mutual-aid societies were in response to pressing day-to-day conditions. In *that* sense, they were political.

Professor August Meier has described the situation in Pennsylvania at the turn of the century:

> . . . a minister was on the board of almost every incorporated business in the state, the largest building and loan association was founded by a clergyman, the great majority of the benevolent and insurance societies and most of the private schools had grown directly out of church activities, a number of the largest political rallies were held in churches, and clergymen were

among the most powerful political leaders, the only
Negro member of the State Republican Committee
being a Baptist minister.[10]

This third type of minister does not focus primarily on
electoral politics, although he is not opposed to such action. His focus essentially is on organization through the
church structure to achieve certain goals mainly of an
economic nature, such as jobs, better housing, better
health care and better educational facilities. He may be
fighting the narcotics problem in the community or using
his church as a base to organize a consumer co-operative.
The SCLC, led by Dr. King and many Southern ministers,
was instrumental in several mass-protest demonstrations in
the South in the late 1950's and early 1960's. The targets
of those demonstrations were racial discrimination in
places of public accommodation, voter registration, jobs
and so on. In many places these campaigns were led by
local preachers and conducted out of the church building
as the headquarters. The Reverend Andrew Young of
SCLC has described the function of the churches in the
South in organizing blacks to protest against segregation
and discrimination in the late 1950's and early 1960's.
Dr. King and the preachers were able to develop a language and a kind of new political theory based on the
religious inclinations and understandings of the local
people. In a seminar at the Metropolitan Applied Research Center in New York on February 1, 1971, Reverend
Young declared:

> . . . it was that religious language. Nobody could have
> ever argued segregation and integration and gotten peo-
> ple convinced to do anything about that. But when
> Martin [Luther King] would talk about leaving the
> slavery of Egypt and wandering in the wilderness of
> separate but equal and moving into a promised land,
> somehow that made sense to folk. And they may not

have understood it; it was nobody else's political theory, but it was their grass roots ideology. It was their faith; it was the thing they had been nurtured on.

And when they heard that language, they responded. You could go into Mississippi and tell people they needed to get themselves together and get organized. And that didn't make much sense. But if you started preaching to them about dry bones rising again, everybody had sung about dry bones. Everybody knew that language. I think it was that cultural milieu, when people were really united with the real meaning of that cultural heritage, and when they saw in their faith also a liberation struggle that they could identify with, then you kinda had 'em boxed. They all wanted to be religious. And when you finally helped them to see that that religion meant involvement in action, you kinda had 'em hooked then. You had a ready framework around which you could organize people. You had people in churches. And usually in the smallest country town, you had people in those churches. And that was what, I guess, gave us kind of key to the first organizing phases.

For about thirteen years Reverend Martin Luther King, Jr., was virtually unrivaled as the major moral and civil-rights leader in the country. Possessing many charismatic qualities, he appealed to both races, unlike the dynamic Malcolm X, who at first appealed primarily to blacks. Both men were black preachers with all the oratorical skills required for that profession, but their backgrounds were profoundly different. King was born and bred in the Southern Baptist tradition in a middle-class black family. Equipped with a good formal education which included the Ph.D. degree, he was able to combine several cultures to move millions to action. He came from the Southern, shouting black Baptist culture, the son of a Baptist preacher. He moved comfortably in Northern intellectual circles, the recipient of considerable financial support from whites who never experienced a black Baptish church service. Rural black people flocked to his mass meetings and followed him on protest marches. Northern white people honored him and saw him as a catalyst to change and a safety valve against black violence. He preached nonviolent struggle at a time when masses of blacks were beginning to act politically. And at all times he combined his Christian theology with social action to achieve what he perceived to be his ultimate goal, "the beloved community." Precisely because of these appeals, King for a time served as the major linkage figure between protesting blacks and white Americans. His involvement in mass protest action legitimized that action in the minds of many whites. But, ironically, it was this legitimation that angered a growing number of younger blacks who no longer sought or especially wanted favor from whites in the human rights struggle. King understood the rising sentiment of Black Power and black consciousness, but he was never willing to conclude with Malcolm X that blacks and whites should form their own separate organizations. In fact, at the time of his death, on April 4, 1968, he was preparing a mass march on Washington which would include Puerto Ricans, Chicanos, American Indians and poor whites.

King sought to use his ministerial skills to mobilize blacks and his theological arguments to win over whites. For a brief time in some places he was successful. His style, substance and goals fitted the historical period. He was, indeed, more effective as a moral leader than as a hard-nosed political bargainer, although he tried constantly to combine the two qualities. It will never be known whether he could have marshaled his influence to bring moral and political pressure to deal with national economic problems as he had done for years in the South in attacking problems of racial segregation.

It is clear, however, that the kinds of moralistic appeals for which King was noted in the late fifties and early sixties were no longer particularly fashionable in the late sixties and early seventies. Many segments in the society, white and black, were becoming less receptive to moral pronouncements. As the civil-rights struggle spread to the Northern cities, many people began to redefine their interests and priorities—black and white people. Like Malcolm X, King undoubtedly was in the process of rethinking his approach and his goals. But it is probably safe to say that he would have remained, fundamentally, a Baptist preacher bent on reconciliation of the races through nonviolent action.

A major example of the type of church-based, programmatic, ministerial action occurred in Philadelphia from 1959 to 1963. Led by Reverend Leon Sullivan (appointed a member of the board of directors of General Motors in 1970), four hundred ministers, operating from their pulpits, conducted several "selective patronage" campaigns against white businesses in that city, campaigns aimed at securing more equitable employment for black people. The ministers met and chose a particular company to boycott unless or until that company agreed to change its employment policies and hire and promote more blacks. The group had negotiating teams as well as resource teams. They investigated the company's circumstances and made a series of demands, and if these demands were not met after a stipulated time, the ministers would take to their pulpits on Sunday morning and announce the campaign. Reverend Sullivan described the operation:

> The spokesman and his team negotiated with the company on the time limit for meeting the request of the four hundred. The minimum was hard and fast and the company was usually given four weeks, sometimes six. But if the executives had been hard to reach

for the initial meetings, the time usually given was two weeks. In several instances, when sincere attempts had been made to meet the requests, an extension was given. But for the most part, when the time had elapsed and the minimum request had not been met, the company executive was informed of the action that would follow, and the ministers were notified by telephone chain or by postcard. On the next Sunday morning the ministers went to their pulpits, and at some point during the service, all four hundred of them invoked Selective Patronage against the particular company, . . . And their congregations would resolve not to patronize that company's products or goods or installations until the minimum requests of the four hundred colored preachers were met.[11]

The preachers relied solely on their pulpits to "call on" and "call off" a campaign. They did not utilize the mass media for the first three years of the action. Sullivan says:

In all, there were twenty-nine Selective Patronage campaigns between the years 1959 and 1963. It has been estimated that as a result of these campaigns in Philadelphia more than two thousand skilled jobs were opened directly to colored workers. Indirectly, the numbers reached several thousands more, because there was a chain effect. A campaign against one company usually resulted in job opportunities for colored men and women throughout an entire industry.[12]

This was a perfect example of black preachers' using their pulpits for political action for benefits for black people. Out of this venture grew Operation Breadbasket under the auspices of SCLC.

It is undoubtedly correct to say that no other institution or leadership group in the black community could have operated with such dispatch and efficiency. The black preacher had in his presence people who would respond to him and who could spread the word immediately. Thus in the 1960's, as throughout black history, the black church was one of the most effective means of mobilization and communication.

It is not unusual to find ministers involving their congregations in social-action programs. Frequently, pastors have asked their members to support boycotts, voting drives, and so on. One thing, however, was unusual about the Philadelphia movement. There is no precedent for such a large number of black clergymen in one city uniting over an extended period of time behind a program of concerted action of this type. The bus boycott in Montgomery, Alabama, of course, was largely minister-led, but the numbers were nowhere near four hundred, and there was extensive local and national press coverage from the beginning.

Another kind of action began in 1970 which was unique in the annals of black preacher-black church action. This involved the decision on the part of a black church in Denver, Good Shepherd Baptist Church, led by Reverend Robert G. Doll, to discontinue the mortgage payments on its church property purchased from another religious group, the (white) Wisconsin Evangelical Lutheran Synod. The property, purchased in December, 1965, for $27,000, was financed by the seller at 6 percent interest and was to be paid off by $150 monthly installments. In April, 1970, Reverend Doll, the chairman of Good Shepherd's deacon board and the church's financial secretary, wrote the Wisconsin Synod:

> In response to an outpouring of the Holy Spirit and as an act of faith and Christian discipleship, we make the following declaration: The Good Shepherd Baptist Church, in a specially called meeting held at 8:00 P.M., Sunday, April 19, 1970, has decided to cease payment on the mortgage for the property located at 2814 Ivy

Street, Denver, Colorado. . . . It is our conviction that the property at 2814 Ivy Street belongs to Almighty God. In His Providence, its care and usefulness have been entrusted to our keeping. Having already been purchased once, we do not feel that it is responsible stewardship for our portion of God's wealth to be utilized for its repurchase. God's House is an Holy Place, not to be bought and sold.[13]

The black churchmen contended that the previous white occupants of the premises sold because they were unable or unwilling to continue their parish in a neighborhood that was changing from white to black. They further stated that the property was overpriced by ten thousand dollars, and it was not correct for one church body to make a profit from another. But the blacks emphasized:

. . . we wish the members of the Board of Trustees (of the Wisconsin Synod) to realize that our decision has been made on moral rather than financial grounds. We are able to continue to pay on the property but have elected to dedicate our $150.00 monthly payments to a special Discipleship Fund. Our resources, which we dedicate to Christ, ought, we feel, to remain within our community to serve His Purposes here.[14]

Thus the blacks had a combination of reasons for taking their action—religious, racial and economic.

Needless to say, the white church group disagreed, and it stated its position in a series of letters from May, 1970, to March, 1971. It subsequently turned the matter over to a lawyer, and an eviction notice was sought. The black group filed a countersuit charging that the whites had inflated the price of the property.

A further argument of Reverend Doll and his associates was that the property was recognized as special religious property by virtue of its tax-exempt status.

A court date was set for April 20, 1972.

This clearly is a pioneering position taken by the black church. It calls into question the nature of private property, contractual relations and religious property held by and transferred among religious groups. The original transaction between the two groups, the blacks argue, was "unScriptural and unChristian as a negotiation to purchase the power of the Holy Ghost." Once the property was originally purchased from a secular source, there should have been no further "sale" of the property to a religious body, except that the subsequent religious buyer would or should have been willing to compensate the first religious buyer for that amount yet unpaid, since "we certainly feel obligated to pay off that which God had not yet allowed them to acquire." In other words, if, say, the Lutherans bought the property for $17,000 and had paid off $10,000, the Good Shepherd Baptist Church would be willing to pay the remaining $7,000, but not a new price of $27,000, or even $17,000, or $20,000. "We feel that it was originally purchased with the resources with which God blessed Pilgrim Lutheran Church. Therefore, we cannot understand how, under Scripture and the Spirit, you can expect God to pay for the property again through us. . . . We affirm that our present contract is an inappropriate way for Christians to relate to one another over that which is our Father's."

The importance of the black position lies in its challenge of established religious views concerning how Christians should relate to each other. It raised a basic *moral* question, not essentially a *civil law* question. There is no known legal precedent the black church can rely on. But it is this type of action that raises new questions of a normative kind for the society to ponder, and it is not unusual to find the black preacher and his church in the vanguard.

Reverend Doll was not unaware of the wider implications of the stand he was taking. This black preacher and his church were raising issues which—whatever the immediate legal rights—were no less significant vis-à-vis the role of religious bodies in social matters than the much publicized Black Manifesto's demand for reparations in 1969. It might be easy to dismiss the action of the blacks on legal grounds, but the moral, religious, racial and economic points raised by the Good Shepherd Baptist Church could not, in the long run, be dismissed so easily. On July 10, 1971, Reverend Doll wrote:

> We do not plan to give up. We will face them in the District Court of Denver on October 20th where they will at least have to explain or justify the inflated price of the property in secular terms. We still feel we are taking a stand which, although odd in our present day, will make increasing sense in years to come—not only in relation to not-for-profit, tax exempt property but in relation to urban land use both in general and in particular.[15]

The New Black Theologians

Beginning with the Black Power movement in 1966, some black clergy in virtually every denomination began to reassess the relationship of the Christian church to the black community. Black caucuses developed in the Unitarian, Catholic, Presbyterian and Episcopal churches. The central thrust of these new groups was to redefine the meaning and role of the church and religion in the lives of black people. Out of this reexamination has come what some have called a "Black Theology." Emphasis is placed on the role of the church as a means of "liberating" people from sociopolitical, economic oppressive conditions in this life. Jesus is seen as a revolutionary. Professor James H. Cone, a black professor of theology, writes:

The Christian Gospel is the good news of the liberation of the oppressed from earthly bondage. If the Gospel of Christ is preeminently the gospel of the liberation of the oppressed, then the theological assessment of divine presence in America must begin with the Black condition. It is only through an analysis of God as he is revealed in the struggle for Black Liberation that we can come to know the God who made himself known through Jesus Christ. Any other knowledge of God is, at best, irrelevant and, at worst, blasphemy. The presence of Black people in America, then, is the symbolic presence of God and his righteousness for *all* the oppressed of the land. . . . Black theology is that theology which arises out of the need to articulate the significance of Black presence in a hostile white world. . . . To study theology from the perspective of Black theology means casting one's mental and emotional faculties with the lot of the oppressed so that they may learn the cause and the cure of their humiliation.[16]

The proponents of this view see the traditional white-oriented church as a racist institution that fails to address itself to revolutionary change and to the alleviation of oppression on earth. They see such a church as essentially the tool of *status quo* powers, and they condemn those black churches and leaders who attempt to emulate white churches.

Black Theology focuses on *community* development more than an *individual* change. In a position paper issued in September, 1969, a group of black Catholic nuns, the National Black Sisters' Conference, stated:

. . . black folk have retained and employed resourcefully those assets which are ours by the grace of God. We black sisters are fully aware of that great *wealth of person* which is the rich heritage of black people in America. We appreciate most deeply that total black experience, that indefinable yet identifiable "soul"

which is our proud possession. . . . These personal
assets in which we glory, and for which we praise and
thank God, are not the sum total of our possessions as
a people. Over and above these is that greatest of all
gifts, that *communal concern* of black folk for their
own people. . . . the communal concern of black folk,
so often misinterpreted and misread as social pathology
in a sick society, is our greatest asset.

Sister M. Martin De Porres Grey stated, "In August, 1968,
the National Black Sisters' Conference was organized to
challenge these nuns to be reborn into involvement in the
liberation of black people as celibate, black and committed
women." [17] (There are 900 black nuns out of a total of
176,341 in the United States.)

The Reverend Albert B. Cleage, Jr., pastor of the Shrine
of the Black Madonna in Detroit, rejects the individualism
of what he calls "slave Christianity":

In the Old Testament and in the Synoptic Gospels,
God is concerned with a people, not with individuals.
Yet, the slave Christianity that we were taught told us
that God is concerned with each individual. And the
master told each slave, "If you are a good slave, God
is going to take care of you and you will be saved." He
didn't tell them that if all you black people love God
and fight together, God is going to help you get free
from slavery. The group concept is historic Christianity.
Individualism is slave Christianity. . . . This was the
emphasis that the slave master wanted to make so that
he could use religion to control his slaves.[18]

The Reverend William B. McClain of Boston also noted
the reliance of black preachers on the Old Testament:

A survey of the biblical texts used by preachers on that
awful Sunday morning in 1963 when the Sixteenth
Street Baptist Church was bombed in Birmingham,

Alabama, killing four young black girls in their Sunday classroom, revealed that the vast majority of Black preachers used Old Testament texts while the white preachers without exception preached from the New Testament. That was not a coincidence. The prophetic word of the Old Testament, announcing judgment on the nation, is often heard in the Black church and applied to contemporary America. Preaching in white churches tends to be of a much more "pastoral" nature, emphasizing individuals and their personal behavior rather than the revolutionary ethic of Jesus and the prophetic judgment on the whole community.[19]

Perhaps one of the most provocative aspects of the Black Theology is the interpretation of Jesus and God as *black*. This involves a new analysis of Christianity. Both Professor Cone and Reverend Cleage see whites as relying on their Christian faith to expiate their sins. Cleage says:

The oppressor, the white man, needs a religion that gives him an opportunity to find escape from the guilt of his oppression. He knows that his oppression is destroying black people all week. He knows that he is responsible for a system of oppression that keeps little black children in inferior schools. He knows that everything he does is designed to reduce black men to permanent powerlessness and inferiority. He needs a religion that can give him escape from these feelings of guilt. His religion has to give him an individual escape from guilt. The white Christian finds the basis for this religion in the New Testament, in the Epistles of the Apostle Paul. He must find escape from the guilt of white racism in a faith in universal brotherhood. This faith provides "escape techniques" for the white Christian, without in any way endangering white power and domination.

A white Christian can go out into the community and do little brotherhood acts. He can fight for "open occupancy." He can do little, almost meaningless acts of face-to-face kindness which in no way touch the problem of the black man's powerlessness. That's his religion.

But our religion is something different. The black man's religion is essentially based on the Old Testament concepts of the Nation Israel, God's chosen people, and our knowledge that the problems of the black Israelites were the same as ours. When we read the Old Testament, we can identify with a black people who were guided and loved by God. Everything in the Old Testament speaks directly to our problem.

We know that Israel was a black nation and that descendants of the original black Jews are in Israel, Africa, and the Mediterranean area today. The Bible was written by black Jews. The first three gospels, Matthew, Mark, and Luke, tell the story of Jesus, retaining some of the original material which establishes the simple fact that Jesus built upon the Old Testament. Jesus was a Black Messiah. He came to free a black people from the oppression of the white Gentiles. We know this now to be a fact. Our religion, our preaching, our teachings all come from the Old Testament, for we are God's chosen people. God is working with us every day, helping us find a way to freedom. Jesus tried to teach the Nation Israel how to come together as a black people, to be brothers one with another and to stand against their white oppressors.[20]

Professor Cone relies on an analysis of God's identification with the struggles of a people to liberate themselves to reach his conclusion that "God is Black."

The blackness of God, and everything implied by it in a racist society, is the heart of Black Theology's doctrine of God. There is no place in Black Theology for a colorless God in a society when people suffer precisely because of their color. The black theologian must reject any conception of God which stifles black self-determination by picturing God as a God of all peoples. Either God is identified with the oppressed to the point that their experience becomes his or he is a God of racism. . . .

The blackness of God means that God has made the oppressed condition his own condition. This is the essence of the biblical revelation. By electing Israelite slaves as his people and by becoming the Oppressed One in Jesus Christ, God discloses to men that he is known where men experience humiliation and suffering.

. . . his election of Israel and incarnation in Christ reveal that the *liberation* of the oppressed is a part of the innermost nature of God himself. This means that liberation is not an afterthought, but the essence of divine activity. The blackness of God then means that the essence of the nature of God is to be found in the concept of liberation. . . . People who want to know who God is and what he is doing must know who black people are and what they are doing.[21]

And what Cleage calls "escape techniques" for white Christians—that is, individual acts of brotherhood and of "face-to-face kindness"—Cone calls "sin offerings." Understanding and accepting the blackness of God, Cone says,

does not mean lending a helping hand to the poor and unfortunate blacks of the society. It does not mean joining the war on poverty! Such acts are sin offerings that represent a white way of assuring themselves that they are basically a "good" people. Knowing God means being on the side of the oppressed, becoming *one* with them and participating in the goal of liberation. *We must become black with God!* [22]

The new Black Theologian believes that the black preacher must, then, be constantly involved in many different kinds of community, political actions: helping to organize blacks, leading protests if necessary, developing "black youth leadership programs."

Several black ministers involved in this new Black Theology movement have stated that they are able to attract many younger blacks to their churches precisely because of the new black-consciousness thrust.

In addition, there is an effort to overcome established denominational divisions. In Chicago in 1970, black Catholic priests celebrated a Mass—they called it a "Black Mass" —where they invited a number of black Protestant ministers to participate, including the Reverend Jesse Jackson.

In 1971, a black reporter for *The New York Times* wrote an article on the new Black Theology in which he stated:

> And in their attempts to shape a black theology, these clergymen from divergent religious backgrounds are also attempting to make their historically divisive denominational ties irrelevant to the new gospel they preach.
>
> "I am a card-carrying Presbyterian—for identification purposes only," said the Rev. Metz Rollins, executive director of the National Committee of Black Churchmen.
>
> And the Rev. Lawrence Lucas, a Harlem-based Catholic priest, said he had more in common with many black, non-Catholic clergymen than with most white priests he knew.[23]

As might be expected, this new black religious thrust is not without its bitter critics and others who cautiously question its content and approach. Reverend Lorentho Wooden, who speaks in Chapter VIII of this book, was an original signer of the NCBC statement in July, 1966. He expresses serious reservations about Professor Cone's views on "the blackness of God."

At any rate, the new attention to a Black Theology is not a minor concern among many black ministers today, and it will probably grow. It has, in addition to the philosophical arguments, a number of attributes attractive to younger ministers and seminarians. It clearly is not part of the stereotype of black worshipers who imitated the whites and concerned themselves only with heaven. It is an active, socially conscious appeal, which requires the minister to become involved in everyday affairs in the political community. It is, to many, assertive, defiant, firm and positive. It provides what many black activists feel is needed: an ideological framework that is both religiously and indigenously black. The new Black Theologians feel they can relate to black people on a new Christian basis, without having to apologize constantly for "white" Christianity or constantly to rationalize the contradictions between what white Christians do and what they profess to believe. The Christianity most whites practice is hypocritical, they say. To understand true Christianity, one must see it through a black perspective.

VI

Conflicts and Criticisms

Dissension and Disagreement in the Pulpit

Earlier, in Chapter I, it was stated that normally one found harmony existing in most black churches, especially between the preacher and the parishioners. And where there was disharmony, it usually did not last long. While this is the *usual* case, one should not get the impression that black churches are virtual palaces of peaceful relations. In fact, some of the most bitter and explosive arguments in the black communities have centered in the churches. Most times these have not been reported in the press, even the black press, but occasionally an especially dynamic or scandalous situation cannot escape being given front-page coverage in the black newspapers or even becoming the subject of a rather extensive feature in one of the black magazines.

For the most part, the arguments do not pertain to doctrine. The basic differences, that is, between the Black Theologians and the traditional black ministers are not matters thrashed out in the media or even from the public platform and pulpit. If ever the adage "You go to your church, and I'll go to mine" is observed, it is applied in this instance. There is no overt, ongoing public dialogue

between preachers or, for that matter, between lay followers of the respective doctrines.

Generally, the major upheavals in the black religious
community center around either personal characteristics,
church property or positions of power in the denomination
or particular church. And in all three types of cases, it is
not unusual for the disagreement to end up in court.

The first type of upheaval—personal dissension—is a very
old one, and there are different situations which fall into
this category. There is a perennial battle in the national
church bodies between those ministers of larger, more af-
fluent churches and those of smaller, poorer congregations.
Obviously, the former are more influential and hold the
top positions, but at times they have been known to complain that the latter not only do not contribute financially
as much as they can, but are an economic drain on the
national body. This matter was hotly debated in the General Conference of the A.M.E. Church in 1892 in Philadelphia. The poorer ministers were accused of coming to
the meeting with insufficient funds to cover their expenses
and thus having to be supported by the General Conference. The Episcopal Address, read by Bishop H. M. Turner, contained the following comments on the problem:

> Our Book of Discipline makes it incumbent upon
> every itinerant minister to collect his traveling ex-
> penses to and from the Annual Conferences. But hun-
> dreds of our preachers appear to be ignorant of this
> requirement; and at the close of our annual sessions
> there are almost invariably a number of preachers pres-
> ent who are unable to leave for their fields of labor
> without being assisted by the Conference, or remaining
> as a burden upon the community for a time, begging
> money to pay their passage home. Nor does the seeming
> helplessness stop there. Presiding elders not infrequently

will bring to the Conference preachers who are candidates for admission, and who are unable to pay their way either back to their homes or to the field of labor to which they are sent. We hope the General Conference will by some legislation put an immediate end to this condition of affairs; and any preacher who is not able to collect his traveling expenses to and from his Conference, let him be instructed to remain at his post and send his report to the Conference by his presiding elder. It is certainly time to put an estoppel on this ministerial mendicancy. Moreover, any preacher who is too devoid of energy to raise his own traveling expenses is generally a dead weight upon an Annual Conference, except in the case of new missions. Thousands of dollars are wasted annually by the Conferences upon that class of mendicant preacher that might be devoted to mission churches at home and mission fields abroad, which would double the membership in a few years and save thousands from everlasting perdition.[1]

This remark brought forth sharp resentment from many preachers in the meeting who felt it was unfair and unjust. The "little men," they felt, were the backbone of the church; they were the ones who had to "beat the bushes," and they were the "real burden-bearers." Frequently, it was answered, they were overtaxed with special Conference fees and simply ran out of the little amount of hard-earned money they were able to scrape together to attend the meeting.

This is still a cause of covert dissension among ministers today. It is not unusual for one to hear preachers from small churches accuse those from large churches of being "high hat" and too "money conscious." They accuse them of measuring worth in the church by the size of the financial contribution rather than by the number of converts or by the strength of faith. One minister of a small Baptist church said, "I just don't have any truck with those high-hat boys, the ones who think that if you don't send thousands of dollars to the national office, you're not worth anything. We send what we can, and I know the Lord will bless us just as much as them."

Another kind of personal dispute involves the morals of the minister. More than a few times, a church has been torn asunder by charges from an individual or group within it that the minister is guilty of acts of immorality. At times, as stated earlier, considerable effort is made to conceal this, to keep it from becoming a matter of widespread knowledge. But this is not always possible. And once the whispers and rumors start, it is very difficult to keep the situation from mushrooming. Frequently, it concerns charges that the minister is having a sexual affair with someone in the church. The minister invariably denies this, and if he wants to protect his name and his position, he might countercharge that the rumors are the work of people who want his job or who have a personal grudge against him.

Very seldom do these cases become matters for press attention. In most instances they are word-of-mouth charges, but if one side files a court suit, as has been known to happen, or if there is a public meeting held in the church on the matter, then the black press will likely report it—in detail. These kinds of situations always receive public attention when a lawsuit is filed, as was the case in a highly sensational incident in Los Angeles in 1954. The minister of a two-thousand-member Baptist congregation was sued by the father of a twenty-year-old girl. The father charged that the minister frequently seduced his daughter over a four-year period and finally abducted her to Gary, Indiana. The major evidence was eight phonograph records made of conversations allegedly held between the minister and the girl, alluding to unnatural sexual relations. The minister denied that his was the male voice on the records, and the girl, who had been the minister's personal secretary, also denied the relationship. But the father was insistent.

The deacon board supported the minister, and the congregation three times voted its confidence in the minister by votes of 663–2, 885–15 and 699–1. Church members argued among themselves, and one filed a suit for slander against another. A nationally circulated black magazine wrote a feature article on the incident, entitled "Trouble in the Pulpit," with pictures of the major contestants. The article stated: "He [the minister] was cleared of involvement in 'lewd records scandal' in church vote which bound members to never bring controversy up again."

In similar incidents, the minister has been known quietly to leave the church, and sometimes the city, after rumors have started.

Another kind of conflict involving personal differences among black ministers developed in 1971 among clergymen in the Presbyterian Church. Reverend Lawrence F. Haygood of Tuskegee, Alabama, went before the 111th meeting of the General Assembly of the Presbyterian Church, United States, and asked the Church's support for a vocational school he had established in Tuskegee. The school, the Southern Vocational College, emphasizes training people, primarily blacks, for jobs which do not require a college education. The request was vigorously opposed by another group of black Presbyterian ministers who saw the school, first, as unnecessary and, second, as a conservative venture, after the fashion of their interpretation of Booker T. Washington, who also started in Tuskegee with emphasis on vocational training.

Both groups of black ministers were members of the Black Presbyterian Leadership Caucus, Reverend Haygood's having served as the first chairman of the Caucus. *The Miami Herald* described the disagreement as a "power struggle" in the Caucus, and said, "The struggle is between 'Uncle Toms' and 'activists,' according to the Rev. Mr. [Snowden I.] McKinnon, who is an activist."

The Southern Presbyterian Church supports one black school, Stillman University in Tuscaloosa, Alabama, a four-year liberal-arts college. Reverend McKinnon felt that Reverend Haygood's school would drain money away from Stillman. It was also believed that the Church should have a more comprehensive educational program for blacks which would be more relevant to the growing needs of a technological society, rather than merely centering on support for one small vocational school in one small Southern rural county. "We will have our fights just like the white folks, I suppose," Reverend McKinnon said. Regarding his relationship with Reverend Haygood, he said, "We remain friends, but I'm going to fight him on this." Haygood had lined up support from many conservative white ministers in the Church, while the white liberals tended to support the McKinnon group. Haygood was firm in his denunciation of the white liberals, whom he felt became very worried when black people "begin to move on their own to help themselves." Haygood admitted that he openly engaged in "ecclesiastical politics," shaking hands and meeting people at the annual meeting. The Assembly agreed to appoint a committee to study the request and to decide on the matter at its meeting in June, 1972.

Conflicts over church property—sometimes money—are rather frequent occurrences in the black church. At times members of a congregation have charged that the pastor has mismanaged church funds. A church in Chicago was hit with this in 1964, and it was revealed that the minister had made a $100,000 donation to a white college in Indiana. The black preacher admitted the donation, but he denied any charges of mismanagement. "Yes, I gave $100-000 to Anderson College in Indiana," the minister stated, "and the school has a building as a memorial named after the Reverend Mr. Dunn [the founder of the black church in Chicago] and a plaque placed where everyone can see it." Some church members petitioned him to resign, but he refused.

The National Baptist Convention, U.S.A., suffered a major split following a conflict over a publishing house in 1915. In 1896, the Convention established a Publishing Board under the supervision of the Home Missions Board. The Reverend R. H. Boyd, corresponding secretary of the Home Missions Board, became corresponding secretary of the Publishing Board. He was an astute businessman and banker, as well as an effective minister. He incorporated the Publishing Board in Tennessee as a separate legal entity apart from the Convention. There was no formal objection to this move at the time. Over the years the enterprise grew substantially, and in nine years it had grossed nearly two-and-a-half-million dollars. Reverend Boyd built a new building for the Publishing Board on land owned by himself, and he also copyrighted all the Board's materials in his own name. In other words, while he made reports to the annual Convention meetings, he clearly viewed the Publishing Board as the property of himself and the Tennessee Corporation. When some members of the Convention attempted to assert control over Reverend Boyd in his operation of the Publishing Board, it was legally too late. He refused to open the books to the Convention's auditor, and in 1915 a split occurred. This gave rise to a new group, the National Baptist Convention of America, Unincorporated, which became known in black church circles as "the Boyd Baptists." The original group had to start an entirely new publishing outfit.

Some ministers are in a position to handle large sums of money, and frequently their control over these funds goes pretty much unquestioned by subordinates in the church. Clearly, bishops in the A.M.E. Church, because of their position and power within their episcopal districts, are able to exercise great authority over the disposition of funds. One of the most bitter and prolonged conflicts in black-church history occurred within the A.M.E. Church from 1957 to 1964 and involved charges of embezzlement and fraud brought against Bishop D. Ward Nichols.

In 1957, charges were brought against Bishop Nichols by another minister along with the president of Edward Waters College, an A.M.E. college in Florida. They alleged misconduct in office, and a trial committee convened by the Church found the bishop guilty. Nichols appealed to the Judicial Council of the Church and the conviction was reversed the following month, September, 1957. In December, 1957, however, Bishop R. R. Wright, president of the Bishops Council, issued a ruling that Nichols must remain suspended until the 1960 General Conference. Wright did not act in the name of the Bishops Council, but no member voted against his ruling.

This last decree prevailed until February, 1958, when the Bishops Council did rule that Nichols could assume his duties as head of the Sixteenth Episcopal District. This district includes New York, Pennsylvania, New Jersey, Delaware, Maryland, the New England states, the District of Columbia, Bermuda and the West Indies. This most recent ruling, therefore, affirmed the September, 1957, Judicial Council decision and overruled Bishop Wright. Nichols was paid three months' back salary. At this point he felt the matter was ended, and he went off to the Virgin Islands to assume his duties. It was Bishop Wright, however, who was greeted in the West Indies and allowed to preach in the A.M.E. churches there, while Bishop Nichols was refused access to the pulpit. He remained less than twelve hours.

In June, 1958, the Judicial Council once again ruled in favor of Bishop Nichols. This ruling was on appeal from a decision by another trial committee in Philadelphia in April, 1958. Some ministers had charged Bishop Nichols with illegally handling church funds, disobedience to the order and discipline of the church and administration, and "placing burdensome assessments upon the Church and brethren for personal gain." The trial committee believed that there was enough evidence to have Bishop Nichols suspended until the 1960 General Conference. The Judicial Council, by a 7–6 vote, disagreed.

At this point, several clergy and lay officials of the Church were becoming weary of the protracted battle, and they could see a possible split in the denomination occurring if the dispute were not settled definitively and quickly. It was not settled, and several clergymen turned to the courts. They charged Nichols with failing to account for approximately $200,000 in funds during the years 1952–56 while he was head of the First Episcopal District. A magistrates court in July, 1958, ordered him placed under $1,000 bail for grand-jury action on charges of fraudulent conversion and embezzlement.

It was alleged that Bishop Nichols created an organization, the Allen Fund Committee, to raise money through the churches for maintenance of the Allen Office Building in Philadelphia. No church body authorized the establishment of the Allen Fund Committee. The property was registered in the name of Bishop Nichols, who had bought it in April, 1949, for $54,020 at a sheriff's sale. Some $16,000 of this money was church funds collected from members of the First Episcopal District. Reverend John D. Bright, secretary of the Philadelphia Annual Conference, was chairman of the Allen Building Fund Committee. Through the churches, some $93,000 was collected for the Allen Building Fund while the property was in Bishop Nichols' name.

Nichols had opened an account ("D. Ward Nichols, Bishop Special") in a Philadelphia trust company. A number of canceled checks amounting to thousands of dollars were presented to the court. These checks, assigned to several A.M.E. clergymen, were allegedly turned over to Nichols, and the clergymen stated that they did not receive any of the money.

When he was indicted, Bishop Nichols stated, "The church courts have thrown out these suits against me. I welcome a chance to produce my audited accounts in any court of my opponents' choosing. My accounts have been audited by a certified public accountant and perhaps now, those who complain will be compelled to take the time to read them."

In 1960, the A.M.E. General Conference suspended Nichols until the entire matter was settled by the courts. But for the next few years, the case was delayed several times. In March, 1964, the trial began in Philadelphia. In addition to careful scrutiny of more than 115 canceled checks, testimony was introduced showing payments to a Richard Allen Community Center in New York. The Center's director was Bishop Nichols' daughter. There were also checks issued to the Book Nook, a bookstore enterprise in New York managed by Bishop Nichols' wife. All the checks were cosigned by Bishop John D. Bright.

In April, 1964, a jury convicted Bishop Nichols of embezzling $100,000 in church funds. This conviction was reversed, however, in November, 1964, by a three-judge court. Bishop Nichols had been charged in the indictment by the African Methodist Episcopal Church Board of Incorporators, a unit of the A.M.E. administration, of which he was a member, and there was no record of its having met as a body since 1928. The three-judge opinion stated that "the Commonwealth offered no satisfactory proof that the funds in the account belonged to the Board of Incorporators of the A.M.E. Church as alleged in all bills

of indictment." There was a "complete lack of evidence
that the funds involved ever came from that source or
that the Board of Incorporators had ever attempted to
exercise jurisdiction over said funds or to require defen-
dant to account for same." No member of the Board of
Incorporators was called as a witness.

In addition, the three-judge opinion stressed the fact
that the act of embezzlement must be accompanied by
secrecy. The special account opened by Bishop Nichols
was generally known, it was not a secret, and Bishop John
D. Bright testified that he was aware of its existence. He
testified that Nichols told him that the account was opened
to protect the funds of the episcopal district from the embarrassment of legal attachments. The Court concluded
that "certainly the account was created openly with the
knowledge if not the approval of the clergy and elders in
his Episcopal District."

And thus a seven-year, highly publicized conflict was
ended.

The cases of "the Boyd Baptists" and Bishop Nichols
demonstrate one striking characteristic. The black preachers at the top of their hierarchical structures are given substantial legal leeway in which to operate. They are able to
enter into contractual arrangements which are not illegal,
and because of the deference paid to them and their positions, they frequently are not questioned in their various
financial operations. When conflicts do develop, it is usually legally too late to do anything about them. They have
secured their legal positions and are usually strong enough
politically within the hierarchy to withstand any attempts
at reprisals from within the denomination. The instances
of property being held in their own names, property purchased with church funds, while clearly not illegal, are
surely practices that would be frowned upon in most other
business arrangements. Therein lies a great part of the

answer. While many of these men are definitely hard-headed businessmen, at the same time they are perceived by the church people as "men of God." Such men are "above" mere mundane, material matters. This attitude has caused no small amount of anguish at times. It is probably the case that more internal accountability should be enforced initially and continuously, and more scrutiny given to the legal operations of the clergy. Some ministers would undoubtedly interpret this as offensive and insulting to their integrity, but that would have to be the risk or price incurred. During the April, 1964, trial of Bishop Nichols, Reverend J. L. Dandridge of Philadelphia testified that he was asked to cash a check for $850 on March 2, 1956. This sum was for travel to the Bishops Council, but this was not explained to Reverend Dandridge by Bishop Nichols. Dandridge stated: "It is the custom in our church not to question the bishop."

Such a custom, to the extent that it exists, reflects at once the power of the top ministers and the source of much of the problems that can lead to bitter conflicts. Proper deference must be balanced by legal accountability.

Inasmuch as the high church positions are so powerful, it can be expected that they will be hotly contested, fights ending, at times, in court. The battle for the presidency of the National Baptist Convention, U.S.A., Inc., was such an incident that began in 1957 and was taken to federal court in 1958. The Reverend Joseph H. Jackson, who was elected president of the organization in 1953, has weathered all challenges, legal and internal, to his leadership, and he has remained the president since his initial election. Elections are held annually at the Baptist Convention.

In 1952, Jackson was vice-president of the Convention and presided over the session that amended the Convention's constitution limiting the president's tenure to four successive terms of one year each. The following year, he was elected president. According to the amended constitution, then, he could serve, upon being reelected, only to 1957. But in the annual meeting in Louisville, Kentucky, in 1957, Jackson was reelected to a fifth term. This set off a major effort on the part of some ministers to oust him, and they filed a suit in the federal court in Washington early in 1958. Their charge was that Jackson was illegally holding office under the Convention's constitution. They also indicated that the conduct of the 1957 Convention was such that confusion and violence prevented any orderly transaction of business.

Reverend Jackson responded that the 1952 amendment was a nullity because it had been considered on the *third* day of the Convention, while the constitution specifically provides that no amendment may be "considered" after the second day of the Convention. When this ruling was made by Jackson in 1957, the rules of the Convention were suspended, and Jackson was reelected by acclamation.

The plaintiffs, ten ministers from various parts of the country supported by affidavits and petitions from hundreds of others, charged that they had been denied access to the platform, that floor microphones had been disconnected, that they had no opportunity to place anyone in nomination, and that when Reverend Jackson made his ruling on the invalidity of the 1952 amendment, there were shouts and screaming, the organ was played, banners were paraded and people knocked aside. Before the demonstration had subsided, a motion was made and carried to suspend the rules and reelect Jackson.

The federal judge ruled in favor of Reverend Jackson, stating that the 1952 tenure amendment was unconstitutionally adopted on the third day. The judge noted the reason for the stipulation that no amendments be considered after the second day: "It was designed to preserve democracy by prohibiting serious action of this kind at a time when many of the delegates from smaller churches, and with limited funds, might have gone home."

As to the charges of confusion and disorder, the judge ruled:

> From my study of the evidence and observation of the witnesses, I must hold that the evidence just discussed was no more persuasive for one side than the other. Nor does it seem of great importance to decide which group was responsible for the disorder. Nor is there sufficient evidentiary basis to hold that respondent Jackson or his representatives were guilty of relators' charge of discrimination in the issuance of admission badges.

The judge stated that he was also impressed by the fact that on the following day after his reelection in 1957, Jackson called for a reading of the minutes of the previous day and asked for a standing vote of approval or disapproval. Approximately five thousand stood in approval, and sixteen voted in opposition.

The matter rested there until the 1960 Convention in Philadelphia. Anti-Jackson forces, supported by Martin Luther King, Jr., Reverend Ralph D. Abernathy and several other prominent civil-rights ministers, backed the candidacy of a popular New York preacher, Reverend Gardner C. Taylor. Reverend Taylor at the time was president of the Protestant Church Council of New York City, the only black member of the New York City Board of Education, vice-president of the New York Urban League, chairman of the Social Action Commission of the Empire State Baptist Convention and pastor of the ten-thousand-member Concord Baptist Church in Brooklyn. It was also very clear that this pro-Taylor group was much more concerned about involving the Baptist churches in social action than

Reverend Jackson was. The group stated that it would establish a lobby in ₹Vashington to fight for civil-rights legislation and work closely with such organizations as the NAACP, the Urban League and the SCLC. Reverend Jackson had made a number of speeches over the years that were considered by many people as taking a more conservative stance on civil rights. Jackson was not in favor of mass-protest action such as marches and picketing. Thus, this battle shaped up not only as a fight to oust a man who many still felt held the office under dubious conditions, but also as a major conflict between the more social-activist ministers and the more traditional or conservative ones.

On September 8, 1960, the Convention's nominating committee, consisting of forty state presidents, had unanimously recommended reelection of Reverend Jackson for his eighth term. This led to a thunderous uproar of protests from the Taylor forces which lasted more than forty-five minutes. During the commotion, the chair ruled that the report of the nominating committee was declared adopted and that this amounted to the reelection of Jackson. The mass uproar continued, and the Taylor forces demanded a state-by-state vote. The Convention officials declared the meeting adjourned and issued a statement later that Jackson had been reelected.

One of the vice-presidents, however, proceeded to conduct a state-by-state balloting and Reverend Taylor received 1,864 votes to 536 for Jackson.

The Jackson forces refused to relinquish the platform to Taylor the following morning. Again, the opposing factions went to court, and, again, Jackson was upheld.

The following year, 1961, at the Convention held in Kansas City, Missouri, the contest erupted again between the Taylor and Jackson forces. Fistfights broke out on the floor, a minister fell from the platform and died of head injuries, and the police had to be called in to quell the ten-minute riot. Jackson was reelected by acclamation.

Since that time, Reverend Jackson has been reelected president virtually without opposition. A short news item in *The New York Amsterdam News* for September 19, 1964, read:

> Detroit—As was widely expected, the Rev. Dr. Joseph H. Jackson glided unopposed into another term as president of the National Baptist Convention, Inc. at a vote by voice election last Thursday at Cobo Arena.
>
> Dr. Jackson, who has served in that office since 1953, and his administrative slate of 19 other officers were elected at the second of five sessions which drew some 10,000 Baptist clergymen and laymen from all parts of the nation.
>
> The unopposed re-election of the Chicago minister was the third straight one since 1961 when he defeated the Rev. Gardner C. Taylor in Kansas City in a contest marked by dissension and sharp rivalry between his supporters and those of Dr. Taylor.

This episode in black Baptist annals has left several ministers highly divided in their feelings. Some feel that Reverend Jackson has provided continuous, sound leadership for the organization and deserves to be supported. Others see an irony in the constitutional stipulation of limiting consideration of amendments to the first two days of the Convention. While the federal judge saw this as contributing to democracy and favoring the smaller churches, one minister stated: "What it really does is let the big boys control things. They can run that convention with a tight fist, and they do."

After 1961, a new group was formed, the Progressive Baptist Convention. This organization consists of ministers and churches who differ with Reverend Jackson's rule of the National Baptist Convention, U.S.A. It is more militant in civil-rights action, and it felt that leaving and forming another group was preferable to remaining and fighting a prolonged battle with the Jackson forces.

Criticisms of the Clergy

In an article in the *Negro Digest* of July, 1963, entitled "Have Negro Ministers Failed Their Roles?," Dr. Nathan Hare, then professor of sociology at Howard University, condemned the old-time black preacher who did little but resort to oratory and exhort his parishioners to fear God. Hare condemned the constant church fights, court battles, the overemphasis on money, and the political silence and inactivity that characterized so many black preachers and their churches. He recognized exceptions, "but these exceptions, as in everything else, are no refutation of the general condition." [2]

These charges, of course, did not go unanswered. A few months later in the same magazine, a black preacher responded, "Negro Ministers Have Not Failed—Have Sociologists?" [3] A great deal of the responsibility for developing the church must be assumed by the parishioners, he argued. Most preachers spend their time caring for the day-to-day needs of their congregation and do not engage in many of the highly publicized church fights and flamboyant activities which hit the press.

But the criticisms of black preachers, generally, have persisted over the years. Those complaints divide black preachers into roughly four categories—those who are materialistic, nonintellectual, authoritarian, or politically noninvolved.

Perhaps the widest criticism, the one heard most frequently in general discussions, is that black preachers are too interested in material things and in conspicuous consumption. Here the flashy dresser riding in long black

Cadillacs, receiving "love offerings" from his congregation, is the image most prominent in the minds of many when they accuse preachers of being materialistic. The emphasis, they feel, is on innumerable collections and fund drives to build big church edifices which seem more to be monuments to the minister than places of religious worship. And this charge is especially strong when the congregation is essentially poor, with many of its members either on public welfare or in the very lowest economic echelon. The hundreds of thousands of dollars spent on building elaborate structures, say the critics, could better be used to develop self-help programs for the poor parishioners. And where the congregation is largely middle-income, the criticism is that the preacher and the church should be less interested in material finery and more concerned about reaching out to help those members of the race economically less well-off. Dr. Hare wrote:

> At the last National Baptist Convention, impressively generous plans were made to purchase 100,000 acres in Liberia, to help Liberian farmers "get on their feet." But only 404 acres were purchased at home, in highly publicized Fayette County, Tennessee, although it doesn't take newspaper headlines to point up needy Negroes. Nary an acre was bought in the big city Northern slums, where droves of Negroes, unlike Liberians, are down on their haunches at the doorsteps of some of the most elaborate church houses in the country.[4]

The fact that *some* churches have done *some* things in this direction is looked upon as not nearly performing up to capacity, that the black preachers and their churches have access to resources which would enable them to do much more in the way of economic development for masses of blacks. One reason for this failure, it is felt, is the intense rivalry and jealousy among ministers—they want to be assured that *they* receive the credit and that *their* positions and churches are not jeopardized.

Another criticism is that black preachers generally are nonintellectual. At times, this is interpreted to mean anti-intellectual, but basically the charge relates to the emotionalism of the minister's appeal and to the fact that many preachers do not have what many would consider adequate formal training. Here, one often hears of the "jackleg" preacher who takes advantage of the usually lower socioeconomic status of his parishioners by playing on their emotions and by engaging in histrionics. Mostly sound, little substance, is the frequent criticism, and while this might be precisely what most of the congregation wants, there is an obligation on the minister to lift the level of understanding and achievement of his people. This is a perennial complaint. An editorial in the *Pittsburgh Courier* in 1940 stated:

> Hollering-preaching won't get it in an age of evolution like this. This is a "thought age" and in order to get men to act, they must be made to think. It is ridiculous for preachers to think that the "Holy Ghost" is the only need to put over God's program. There is a great responsibility resting on the Negro preacher who must finance the church and have charge of its business interests as well as preach, edify and save souls. For this important post, the preacher should be the best informed of all professions. . . . But the Negro church particularly neglects this duty.[5]

The charge of nonintellectualism also is accompanied by the complaint of overemphasis on the next-worldly life. It is a simplistic approach, relying on a religion of fear, constantly to admonish people to live in a way that will get them to heaven and avoid the fire of hell. That is, the literal interpretation of the Bible is seen as unintel-

ligent, and very many black preachers confine their sermons to a literal reading of the "good book." In other
words, while they are materialistic in matters pertaining
to personal comfort, they are otherworldly and academ-
ically weak when it comes to a philosophical understanding of the teachings of Christianity.

The criticism of being authoritarian is one most usually
heard from those persons who are not members of a
church. In fact, it is a reason frequently given for not be-
longing. "That preacher rules things from top to bottom."
"He's a tyrant who makes sure that nothing gets done
without his say-so." Very often the preacher is the only
full-time person devoting himself to the business of the
particular church; all others are part-time and volunteers.
This means that the minister is the overseer of every activity. He prepares the budget, keeps the books, pays the
bills, schedules extra events and invites outside speakers
and choirs. His office is at the church, and only he, along
with a handful of deacons and trustees, has a key to the
building. Even when there are several assistant ministers,
the pastor is their boss, who can hire and dismiss them on
recommendation—a procedure usually followed—to the
deacon board. More than a few persons have commented
on the lack of democratic rule within most black churches,
but, as can be expected, most ministers would deny that
they govern in such a manner.

The charge of authoritarianism is normally associated
with descriptions of the minister's various techniques for
manipulating and controlling the congregation. He will
use his position in the pulpit to reprimand "blacksliders"
and those who are opposed to a particular decision of his.
He will preach a sermon heavily sprinkled with a mixture
of religious references and personal digs. He will deny
access to the pulpit to any who disagree with him. In the
pulpit, he is not only the preacher, but also the prince

who presides largely unchallenged. When this authority *is* challenged, it leads to a conflict which is quickly—in most cases—settled. Some preachers have been known to demand a contract from the church for a stipulated period of time. When this happens, and a major conflict develops, the preacher is known to threaten court action if an attempt is made to remove him. Many preachers have stated that they would prefer to rely on their personal attraction than on a contract, and if they are particularly strong-willed, this could mean relying on various oligarchical techniques to maintain their positions. They might threaten to resign, which is a known technique of the oligarch, who attempts to establish the feeling that the masses simply cannot live without him. They might strongly hint that a bank loan then pending or contemplated might not be approved if the church shows signs of dissension with the minister. The preacher starts out with a heavy presumption of integrity and good faith if only because of his position. It is difficult, in most cases, to overcome that presumption and to prevail against him when he really proceeds to assert his authority, prestige and influence.

Finally, a criticism being heard more and more, especially from younger blacks and from the new Black Theologians, is that most black preachers do not utilize their positions in the black communities to provide the necessary political leadership so badly needed. It is often stated that many secular officials realize the leadership potential of the ministers better than the ministers themselves. The preachers, the charge goes, content themselves with preaching "nonsocial gospel" sermons on Sunday, visiting their parishioners during the week, attending innumerable church-committee meetings dealing with trivia and generally being a big fish in a little pond. They are not any of the three types of activists described in Chapter V, and they do not strive to be.

The politically noninvolved preacher maintains an absolutely separate relationship between church and state. And this, critics insist, is a luxury black people cannot afford. An institution as pervasive in the lives of a people as the black church has an obligation to address itself to the many secular as well as religious problems facing those people. On May 19, 1971, Huey P. Newton of the Black Panther Party, whose father was a minister, made a speech at the Center for Urban-Black Studies in the Graduate Theological Union in Berkeley, California. In his talk, he called for his party to work with the black church, but he stated:

> Now without judging whether the church is operating in a total reality, I'll venture to say that if we judge whether the church operates in a situation of relevance to the total community, we would all agree that it does not. That is why you develop new programs and become more relevant so your pews will be filled on Sundays. . . . Then if we really get ministers who will deal with the social realities that cause the misery, so that we can solve them, so that man will become larger and larger, then their God within will come out, we can see it and merge with it.

All these criticisms are ones heard from many different sources within the black communities. They do not come forth, for the most part, in blazing headlines or dynamic lawsuits. And for each complaint, there is a counter that it is dangerous to generalize, that for each materialistic minister, one can find a self-denying one. That for each nonintellectual, one can point to one who, if not seminary-trained, certainly has studied his Bible carefully. That for each authoritarian, there is the true democrat. That the civil-rights movement was and continues to be substantially supported by the preachers. What all this means, probably, is that a profession so visible and prominent in the community's life is especially vulnerable to criticism when such a large absolute number—notwithstanding their counterparts—fits the charges leveled.

The fact is, of course, that except for the denominations that exercise some hierarchical control over the local ministers, it is very difficult to deal with those cases where the criticisms are valid. This is essentially a function of the relationship between the preacher and the parishioners. Thus, in many ways, the criticisms must be aimed as much at the particular church as at the minister. He is so much a part of the church that he could hardly exist for long in any manner without the sanction of a substantial portion of that church. In virtually all the scandals involving ministers reported in the press over the years, there have been a rather considerable number of his parishioners who have supported each minister. In fact, in some instances, an attack on the minister, especially from outside the church, has been construed by some members as an attack on the parishioners themselves.

The criticisms, furthermore, are usually against "preachers" or "the ministry." The particular church members do not construe this to mean *their* pastor. *He* is not guilty of those generalized charges, whatever might be the case with some other preachers.

VII

Some Problems over Disagreement of Roles

While normally the preacher and his parishioners understand each other and live up to clear expectations of roles,
there certainly are instances where this understanding
does not prevail. Some black preachers have found themselves in rather serious disagreement with their congregations over the proper role of the pastor. This situation
usually occurs when the minister is inclined to be a social
activist, when he wants to involve himself, and frequently
his church, in civic action.

This occasional tension has been noticed more often
in recent years, particularly since the late 1950's and 1960's
with the political activism of such ministers as Dr. Martin
Luther King, Jr., and his associates in the Southern Christian Leadership Conference. In addition, as a minister in
the Nation of Islam (Black Muslims), Malcolm X left his
impact on many younger black ministers.

Reverend Lorentho Wooden's experiences as the rector
of a small church in New Rochelle, New York, St. Simon's
Episcopal Church, are illustrative of some of the problems
that can and do develop between pastor and parishioners.
Father Wooden served that church from 1965 to July,

1971, when he became assistant to the Diocesan Bishop for Urban Affairs in New York.

Born in 1927 in Daytona Beach, Florida, Wooden grew up in the A.M.E. Church, coming from a strongly religious, "Bible-quoting" family. He switched to the Episcopal Church during his seminary years at the University of Chicago. But he stated that the bulk of the black membership of the Episcopal Church in this country is West Indian, and this is a significant fact in understanding the role of the minister and the expectations of the members. Father Wooden explained:

"The strength of the Episcopal Church in America with blacks is—and I'm going to put it in a dramatic form—that it is still a peasant church. It is still West Indian. It is not *American* black. *American* blacks are still Baptists and Methodists. The Episcopal Church is the Anglican Church. In the eastern United States, especially, it is almost always West Indian—I'm talking about for blacks—and almost always an immigrant church.

"In other words, the black West Indian people who come here are thrifty, smart, et cetera. Almost without exception, they come from rural backgrounds and some are educated or get educated here. They're not averse to learning. But to them, at home, on the islands, the Episcopal church is like the Baptist church. That's where everybody went. Ain't no big thing. And they're not impressed with a whole lot of learning from the minister in the pulpit. They will sit there, because that's what they've been taught to do. But they don't really listen to what you have to say. One of my biggest problems now is that the kind of preacher I am—trying to live in the Bible and understand the methods of the Bible and to relate it to an analysis of current American high-powered technological society is for the birds. Because they don't listen to that. They can't hear it."

Wooden wanted his pastorate to be up-to-date with dynamic political, social and economic changes in the society. He believed that as a minister, he should be involved as an active participant in protesting injustices, and he tried desperately to solicit the support and cooperation of his parishioners.

One good example of his efforts developed in New Rochelle in 1966. An urban-renewal plan was being implemented in the downtown section, which included a new shopping center. Macy's department store, along with several smaller businesses, was building a shopping mall. The number of black workers on the construction project was minuscule. "Here was something that was clear," Wooden said. "Macy's started building, and there were no Negroes being employed and all that money on jobs would be available. I had been here about a year. This was a chance to get my feet wet."

Protest demonstrations were mounted, involving several ministers in town. Trucks coming to the construction site were blocked; many ministers and other demonstrators were arrested from time to time. Streets were blocked off and mass marches were held. There was chanting and shouting of protest slogans. Father Wooden was in the forefront, in the marches, in the strategy sessions and on the various community panels called to discuss the protest. Quickly, however, he realized the lack of support from his own congregation; they would not join the mass marches, and many objected to his participation. He declared: "Well, the first thing that really dawned on me was that I couldn't get anybody out of my church to come down. *They wouldn't come down there!* And furthermore, I started getting feedback from some of the people like 'You ought to be ashamed of yourself. You're a minister of Christ.' This was behavior not fitting to a minister, as they understood it. You know, hollering, 'Freedom,' down the middle of the street. Oh no. Hollering and screaming. No. That did not fit their image of the ministry."

Sunday after Sunday from his pulpit, Father Wooden urged his parishioners to join him in the protest. But to no avail. He would try to relate his involvement in protest action to the growing protests among young college people, but he could not persuade his people. The weekly attendance at church suffered. "And the membership did drop off some," he recalled. "Funny. They sort of stayed away, because I had an acid tongue in those days. The whole black thing; I was trying to interpret it. I used to be wringing wet from preaching. I was wailing. . . . Well, it was all to naught. My people in my church did not understand what I was doing."

He analyzed part of the problem as stemming from the national composition of his church. His membership was overwhelmingly black, West Indian, and he is a native American, Southern black.

"I guess," he said, "what I'm saying is that the social-action interpretation of the ministry is not what my people want, necessarily. I have not yet pastored an American native black church. The West Indian is dealing with a whole different image of the ministry."

Father Wooden definitely believed that there was a prejudice among the West Indian toward American blacks, especially against Southern American blacks. The West Indian envisions himself as more militant, more energetic, smarter, and more ambitious than the native American black. Wooden frequently was confronted with this stereotyped view from some of his members. He commented: "The other day, I heard this. And I said, 'Look, I'm tired of hearing this. Now, listen to me good.' I said, 'The group of West Indians who came to this country are natural-born hustlers. Otherwise, they wouldn't be here. And like hustlers everywhere, they know they don't have anything to fall back on. So they just *go!* Dig it! If you go back where you came from—Trinidad, Montego Bay—or wherever it is, you'll find the lazy ones there. And if you go back where I came from, to Daytona Beach, you'll find the lazy ones there, drinking wine, et cetera. I have more in common with you than I have with the cat I left back in Daytona Beach.'

"In other words, as a group, the West Indian in this country is thrifty. He came here for a point. To make it financially. To get out of that grinding poverty. And they have done that. And to come here and look at all American blacks and say they are all lazy is not fair. I tell them, 'You have to separate them out, as we have to separate you out from those you left back home.' "

But he is not optimistic that he persuaded his members. They expected him to act a certain way, that is, to stay in the pulpit and to tend to the business of the church. In addition, Wooden firmly believes that his West Indian congregation had trouble reconciling its stereotype of a lazy American Southern black with the drive and hustle he showed. He declared: "But part of my problem in my present church comes from the fact that I am an American black, and I don't fit their image of a lazy American Southern black. I'm a hustler. And if they don't pay me enough money, what do I do? I get myself an additional job. Well, they understand that hustling, you see. And it troubles them because I'm suppose to be, like, lazy."

His members could, in fact, accept his getting other jobs to supplement his income, but they could not accept the rather "undignified" role of a protest demonstrator in the streets. This was not in keeping with the goals of thriftiness and ambition they held; their vision related more to individual efforts of making money, not to collective, political efforts of overcoming social injustices. Sensing this, Father Wooden stated that it was best that he minimized his social-protest activities in order to avoid a split within his church. And he wonders if his ministerial style and orientation would fit better with a native American black congregation.

"That whole thing," he explained, "of trying to understand and to move along with that revolution was something that was not indigenous to most of the people I was pastoring. I got very little encouragement, and some thought that I was wasting too much time. So I had to pull back just to save the thing, in part. . . . My church down South [Wooden's first pastorate was in Florida] was West Indian. Furthermore, I think the native black American might be able to dig my rhythm a little bit more."

Another kind of problem of role disagreement is illustrated by the case of a black Catholic priest in Detroit, Father Donald Clark. After serving in an all-white parish for a few years in Ypsilanti, Michigan, Clark asked to be assigned to a black parish in the late 1960's. This decision turned out to be a mistake. Clark said: "I had some great fantasies about who I was, and what I was, and what I was ready for. So I thought I was ready to come into the city and be sort of the Malcolm X of the Roman Catholic Church. That was really one of my fantasies about myself, because I had read his autobiography, and I was very much impressed with him. And with his ability to relate to what they call the 'street people.' I really began to conceive of my role in the Roman Catholic Church, what his role had been among black people in general. . . . I found out it was a terrible mistake."

It was a mistake, because Father Clark did not have the background or leadership inclinations of Malcolm X. Clark was essentially middle class in upbringing, training and orientation. He was put off, if not shocked and offended, by the language of little black children on the streets of his parish. "I began to understand that the way

I instinctively reacted was not the way most of the people who lived in the community reacted. So it got to be such a problem for me making a cultural adjustment, that I became less and less happy and retreated more and more from the situation."

He stayed at the parish fourteen months. It was a parish that required a great deal of help with social problems—dope addiction and financial matters, among others. And Clark was unable to be that kind of priest. Although he was initially impressed by Malcolm X, he soon realized that he did not have the mass-leadership skills to emulate Malcolm X. "I was not trained as a social worker, and I wasn't flexible enough to make the adjustment that was required. I just retired from the scene altogether."

After taking a year off, he was assigned in 1970 to a middle-class black parish, Holy Ghost Parish. But this assignment has not answered some basic questions for the thirty-seven-year-old priest, especially concerning what his role should be. He does not want to be "the leader" of his congregation. He feels he should make a determined effort to become a part of the community, but he insists that his talents include only certain theological, intellectual insights "in the theological education area and worship area." He agonizes over what his relationship to his people should be. He perceives himself as defective in many respects, but he is not quite sure if these defects stem from the fact that he might be a "bad priest" in an alien situation or from his defects as a black man unable to assume leadership responsibilities. He sees the question of the role of the black priest in the Church today as a crucial one for which he has no answer, "and that makes me very uncomfortable, not having an answer."

So he attempts to deal with the problem on a day-to-day basis, but his approach is not shared by some of his parishioners. He wants them to assume considerable responsibil-

ity for developing programs in the parish, but they resist
this and insist that that is his leadership role. He is, in a
real sense, an embattled priest. The question of his role
as a priest concerns him intensely, but he has not found
answers.

"So, what I do in the meantime is, I don't really answer
that question," he said. "I don't sit around and try to con-
ceptualize on that level. I say, 'OK, here at this parish, if
we're going to continue to exist in any fashion, it is going
to be because the people here have a will to exist, and
because they have the tools to insure their own existence.'
Which mans that my job here is not to let them put upon
me the responsibility of being the leader in this parish.
And I refuse to do that. I refuse to be the leader. And so
I keep saying to them, 'You want this parish to exist, then
you must make it exist. And I'm here to kick you in the
rear end; if you want theological reasons why this ought
to be, to give you whatever theological insights I might
have. If I have motivational powers, then I'll try to motivate you. I'll do whatever I can, but I'm not going to be
the leader here.'

"And so, rather than sit around conceptualizing my
role in some kind of abstract way, it seems to me that
specifically, my job is to make sure that the rings of power
get transferred out of this house into the hands of the people. So that if a finance committee is going to exist, it is
going to know everything there is to know about parish
finances—where the money is, how to make budgets, what
the expenses go for, and so forth. If there's an education
committee in this parish, they're going to know how to
educate young people, the kids, for First Communion, if
they're interested in that. That may be a grandiose plan;
I'm not so sure that's a for-real thing.

"I think what the people keep telling me is, 'That ain't
for real, Father, because we've got kids to raise, and jobs

to go to, and houses to maintain. And now you want to put this on us, too. That's your job.'

"And I keep saying, 'But that's your job, because the church is part of your life.' "

Black Catholic church members tend to continue to understand the role of the priest as one who takes a rather firm lead over the parish. Father Clark has become influenced by a new emphasis on broad-based participation by the community. He was part of an initial group of black priests which formed in the late 1960's and attempted to address itself to major problems of the Catholic Church's relation to black people. This group formed the Black Catholic Clergy Caucus, and for a year and a half Clark served as the president. This experience apparently inculcated a new sense of the need to approach membership involvement in religious matters in ways different from the traditional order. While Clark has by no means answered many of the problems presented by this new ethos, he clearly perceives the need to redefine his role as a priest. And this is a need obviously not shared by many church members in his parish.

In many ways the experiences of Wooden and Clark are similar. Both perceive the need to modify the role of the ministry, to make it more activist, less pulpit-oriented and more involved in sociopolitical and economic problems. It was Wooden who bluntly stated that the church building per se might be irrelevant today. By this he meant that his role as a minister might best be served by going to a school-board meeting or to some other place where "you can see some of your interested parishioners or maybe to a dance or a social occasion or where you may get into some polemic over some important issue, always trying to put forth a biblical point of view as one of God's children."

Wooden's and Clark's situations are characterized by congregations that are hesitant to participate in the innovative approaches the pastors advocate. This is not uncommon. Frequently the black preachers have found themselves ahead of their parishioners in civic matters.

Very many black people go to church not to become civically and politically active, but out of habit and for purely religious and social reasons. They do not want to be cajoled into social action; they want a minimum of personal bother. In a sense, a minister who makes activist demands on them threatens them, and they are apt to withdraw from *that* church, if not from *the* church, if he persists.

This is an important factor in analyzing the preacher's capacity to be a more effective leader. Very frequently, critics of ministers state that the preachers do not provide nearly the amount of community leadership their positions warrant. This is undoubtedly true in many cases, but it is also true that very many black congregations are far more conservative in their outlook than their ministers. Frequently the average age of the congregation is older than that of the minister; and they are less educated and not as sophisticated about civic involvement as the preacher. Many, indeed, are very involved in church activities, but in the realm of social action, the average black church member is still cautious and somewhat conservative. Thus an otherwise action-oriented Father Wooden must move carefully in politicizing his members. Father Clark must develop the enormous patience that is required to have his essentially tradition-oriented parishioners take a new view of their personal involvement in church and community affairs on a collective basis.

Many churchgoing black people continue to see the church as a haven from the pressing hassles of day-to-day life, and they want to use the church as a place to relax and to worship. One member of Wooden's church in New Rochelle stated: "He [Wooden] didn't realize that many of us were just plain tired after working all week trying to make a living. You just can't ask a person to pick up and go march on Saturday after he's put in long hours all week on a job. Frankly, that's why I didn't march."

The astute black preacher recognizes this, and he knows just how far and how hard to push his members. It has been this sensitivity that has helped sustain the leadership role of the preacher for centuries. One of the major weaknesses of newer, younger leadership groups in the black community is that they have not been able to cultivate the patience necessary to build a mass following and to sustain it over a long period. Preachers have understood that in building mass movements, patience can be a virtue, rather than an attitude that sanctions delay out of an inclination for conservatism and moderation.

Still another situation of disagreement over role occurs when the preacher does not particularly ask his members to involve themselves, but his own actions are such that he is criticized. In such instances, he may be doing things that the members do not see as essentially related to his ministerial duties in the church. This does not mean that he is overly involved in the local ministerial alliance, because this kind of activity usually does not, in any way, interfere with the performance of his duties as pastor of the church. Neither is the criticism too vociferous if the minister takes another job in order to support his family. It is always preferred that this not happen, but in small churches, as with Father Wooden's St. Simon Episcopal Church in New Rochelle, the members realize that the minister must supplement his meager salary with outside employment. Thus, when Wooden took a second job in Harlem working full-time with a narcotics-rehabilitation agency, his parishioners might not have preferred that he spend his time in this way, but they clearly understood the economic necessity for his doing so.

Occasionally, however, one finds a minister engaged in

an extrachurch activity which does not coincide with what many members of his congregation feel he should be doing. The additional activity is not primarily to supplement his income, but is explained by the minister as an endeavor he feels is a logical extension of his Christian work.

An example of this kind of situation is found in Tuskegee, the county seat of small, rural, but developing Macon County, Alabama. This is the home of Tuskegee Institute, founded by Booker T. Washington. There is also a major Veterans Administration hospital there. (The bulk of the staffs of these two institutions is black.) Reverend Lawrence Haygood is the young pastor of Westminister Presbyterian Church, which has approximately ninety members. He went to the church in December, 1965, after serving churches in Virginia and Memphis. Most of the members of his present church are middle-income professional employees of the college or the hospital.

Haygood founded the Southern Vocational College in Tuskegee in 1970. Some members of his congregation felt that the new school would conflict with Tuskegee Institute. Others felt that the establishment of such a school by their pastor was not in keeping with their conception of the proper role of either the minister or the church. Haygood disagrees on both counts. He explains, "This college is not in conflict with Tuskegee Institute, because we're not offering baccalaureate degrees. We have three-month programs, six-month programs; we have two-year programs. And all of them are geared to the student that Tuskegee Institute discards and throws away. That's the student that we are working with."

Growing up in Macon, Georgia, Haygood frankly admits his disappointment with what he calls the "traditional church." This is a place where people go on Sunday and "have a soul-stirring experience," but there is a failure to relate the Christian teachings to the rest of their lives. "No one ever came out to try to teach us in voter registration or to enable us to become politically involved. No one was concerned too much from the church about medical care for persons. No one was concerned about even getting persons out of destitute circumstances to send them on to college."

Reverend Haygood's Southern Vocational College teaches rudimentary skills, secretarial science, practical nursing, bookkeeping. He decided on the need for the school after he assumed the pastorate at Westminister.

"When I came to Tuskegee," he said, "I came here looking for one thing, and behold, I discovered another. I had been aware, you know, of the great books of Booker T. Washington and other educators, and I felt that it was an institution that was really out doing business for that man who was at the bottom of the totem pole. And when I got here, I found a group of middle-class folk working at the Institute who were fairly satisfied themselves and comfortable, with almost no concern about that man who is farthest down that they often mention and that certainly Booker T. Washington was concerned about, and Dr. George Washington Carver. I looked out and I expected people to be exposed to the trades, particularly disadvantaged people who were not looking for a regular four-year college education. But persons who just wanted to learn a trade, so that they can become employed in this technological society in which we live. And I didn't see it."

As accurate as this may be, some members of Reverend Haygood's church would not agree that the church or the minister should get involved in rectifying this situation. One person explained, "That's a job for educators, not preachers. The work of the church, the basically religious work, is enough to occupy full-time."

Haygood combines the two functions: "I see no contradiction between doing these things and the role of the church. In fact, I conceive of that as being the role of the church. It seems to me that persons were serving a God who was a God of justice, a God of love, a God of compassion, then it seemed to me that if they were going to be followers of this God, then they should go out and be instruments of His love, of His compassion, of His justice —by emptying their lives into the lives of their fellow-man."

He combines religion and education at the Southern Vocational College. Church services are held at the school during the week for the students. A major premise of his approach is that "there's a direct relationship or correlation between deep spiritual commitment and job efficiency." In other words, he believes that "religion is the strongest motivation of persons that we have." He believes that those in his church and outside who oppose his work at the school have not fully understood this. He says that he was religiously motivated by God through Jesus Christ to establish the school, and he points to other people, like the Texas billionaire H. Ross Perot, who were religiously motivated to pursue their work.

In spite of this explanation, it is accurate to say that some of his members who oppose his work do so because they feel he will end up devoting a disproportionate amount of his time to the school and not enough to the church. And admittedly, they want to avoid any possible conflict with Tuskegee Institute. They would probably not disagree, or at least not debate, with him on the issue of religious motivation.

In all three instances cited in this chapter, the cases involved preachers who sought more involved roles for themselves and, at times, for their members. Out of this came a disagreement of roles. Not once in the several talks

I held around the country with ministers was there the instance in which the members urged the pastor to take a more activist role against the latter's inclination.

Another observation should be made. One finds most disagreements over role perception occurring in churches in white denominations: Episcopal (Wooden); Catholic (Clark); Presbyterian (Haygood). These black churches appear to display more uncertainty about role definition than churches in the black denominations. This is probably not accidental. The former churches are in greater flux today, generally, than the latter, in redefining their Christian faith, relating that faith to black people, and redefining the relationship of the black preacher to the hierarchy in the denomination and to his parishioners. There appears, in other words, greater certainty, if not greater effectiveness, on these issues in the black denominations. The black denominations, indeed, are not necessarily more effective in doing the work that Reverend Haygood advocates. In fact, when Haygood speaks of the "traditional church," he is probably referring to the church of his childhood, the black Baptist church. But there seems to be a stronger, better established understanding of roles in the black denominations. It is not that the pastor and the parishioners expect less or more from each other. Rather, they have had a longer time to deal with the questions of various roles and have probably worked them out not only to mutual understanding, but to mutual satisfaction. In other words, there may well be a valid point to Wooden's comment that a native, black American church and membership might "dig my rhythm" more.

Finally, the Reverend Kelly O. P. Goodwin, pastor of Mount Zion Baptist Church in Winston-Salem, North Carolina, stated: "The black preacher has always been more free than the white preacher. The white preacher has to be careful about what he says, because he may have big, important white people in his parish. This is not so with the black preacher. The black parishioners do not care what the black preacher says or does as long as he is a good pastor. He can knock the *status quo,* because his people are not really the *status quo* powers."

This statement is generally true, but there are instances, as shown in this chapter, where the black preacher must guard his words and actions. It is true that the *"status quo* powers" are not his members, but at the same time he must be sensitive to other constraints on him from his congregation. While he may "knock the *status quo,"* he must do so consistently with his parishioners' notions of what constitutes a "good pastor." Wooden's members were undoubtedly as opposed to job discrimination as he was, but there could be serious disagreements over the "proper" way a minister should proceed to fight that condition.

VIII

Variety of Experiences with Formal Training

Two of the greatest compliments one can pay a black preacher are that he "knows his Bible" and he "can really preach." His knowledge of the lessons in the Bible need not come from formal training; in fact, a few ministers, usually elderly, to whom I talked virtually boasted of the fact that they "never had a day of real schooling." This was as much a boast about self-dependency and the ability to overcome obstacles as it was clearly an attempt to show an absence of any inferiority complex as a result of having little formal education. For the most part, however, it is correct to say that at the present time, a large percentage of black ministers, especially the younger ones, feel it is essential to have some formal seminary training. There are, of course, a number of reasons for this attitude. Many believe that much can be learned from such study; they respect the fact that there are gaps in the self-taught approach which weaken one's ability to be an effective preacher. Some clearly see the prestige value attached to being able to list the formal training as part of one's credentials. One can see many church bulletin boards listing the string of academic and honorary degrees after the pastors' names.

Very frequently, my mother would tell me that "Reverend Johnson went to the University of Chicago." As a preteen growing up on the South Side of Chicago, I was not quite sure what this meant in terms of courses and degrees, but the University had a distinct image of excellence among my peer group, and anyone who attended had the reputation of being "smart." And at the same time, when the minister did not "flaunt" his education, that is, when he did not act "uppity" or "as if he were better than other people," then this was an added indication of his intelligence. On more than a few occasions, I was reminded that "Reverend Johnson has college sense and common sense."

It was always clear that there was a very important balance to be struck between "being educated and being like ordinary folk." This is a long-standing, serious matter in the black community. On the one hand, there is the constant admonition to "get yourself an education"; on the other, there is the history of many educated blacks' not wanting to associate with lower-class, unskilled members of their race. There has been a continuing attempt in many black circles to combine what might be called class and mass. This is a subject many black preachers will address themselves to very readily. They, more than any other professional group in the black community, have had to deal with it, inasmuch as their daily contacts are with the masses of blacks on a broader basis than the contacts of any other formally trained segment of the black community, except public school teachers—and the latter's contacts are pretty much confined to the children.

One young minister in Winston-Salem, North Carolina, discussed this phenomenon. Reverend Henry Lewis is a professor and chaplain at the predominantly black Winston-Salem State University. He is also pastor of Mount Pleasant Baptist Church in that city, his hometown. His

formal education included undergraduate training at Winston-Salem and a B.D. degree from Andover-Newton in
Massachusetts. (In 1971, he was also taking courses in the
local university graduate school toward a master's degree.)
He was aware of the hesitancy some blacks have toward a
minister who is "too educated."

"Many of our people," he said, "have been oriented
around the idea that if the minister is called, then all this
education we're getting isn't necessary. God will give you
what you need. And with this education, you get over
our heads. You come with an educated sermon, and nobody can understand you. And one of the things I'm proud
of in my church is in this teaching emphasis, that I have
had people on the lower end of the educational scale to
compliment me on the fact that they have understood.

"My grandfather taught me that. He probably hardly
went further than the third or fourth grade. He said to me,
'Son, you've got a lot of education, now. You've been to
college. You've been off up there to Boston.' You know,
he didn't understand why all that was necessary. But he
recognized the fact that I'd been there. And he put his
hand out like this. And he said, 'Now, you're going to have
people in the church, you're going to have a man up here
that is probably got as much education as you've got. He
might have the highest degree. And then on down, you're
going to have people till you get down here to this fellow
like me who has nothing.' And he said, 'Now when you
get in your pulpit to speak, don't you speak to this fellow
up here at all. You speak so I can understand it down here,
and he'll—up here—get it.'

"I don't know, but it was a tremendous illustration in
terms of being relevant to people. So I speak to the uneducated, the illiterate. I try to apply and use words—I go
to great lengths sometimes to get a definition of a word.
Even if I use a theological term that they don't function

with, I take time to say what I mean by that. And give a practical illustration that they can latch onto. They appreciate this; they want this. And I see this as a kind of calling.

"So that probably when people say that they don't want an educated man, they are afraid that he's going to speak above their heads. And that what he says will not be interpreted by them. They can't digest it. They've had this experience; they've seen this happen. They've had ministers come in who were 'educated,' and they say he gives a lecture. 'And we don't want that.' "

Reverend Lewis described this combination of education and an ability to communicate as a "calling." By that he meant a kind of natural talent to relate, to be meaningful and relevant to masses of black people who in all likelihood do not have the level of education needed to understand a college lecture presented in abstract, theoretical terms.

Another Baptist minister in Harlem described the favorable experiences he was having as a graduate student in the School of Social Work at New York University. Reverend O. B. Dempsey is pastor of the Upper Park Avenue Baptist Church, located in a converted five-story bank building at 125th Street and Park Avenue in Harlem. He has spent over twenty years fighting dope addiction and the narcotics traffic in Harlem. He started his ministerial career in Brooklyn, served as an officer in the local NAACP, and worked with youth groups. In 1955, he joined Adam Clayton Powell's Abyssinian Baptist Church in Harlem as director of the boys' club and later became director of the church's community center. Several years ago, he organized the Anti-Crime and Anti-Narcotic Committee of Harlem and New York City. He is noted in the black community as a relentless fighter against narcotics.

"It was about twenty-two years ago when I saw a youngster out there die from an overdose. At that time, it wasn't a good thing to talk about narcotics, because nobody would even discuss it." But Reverend Dempsey persisted. He organized and led mass marches locally and in Washington. He spent six weeks in London in 1964, studying the British approach to the problem, which he called a failure. And he vehemently accused officials of not doing enough in this country to deal with the problem.

"During the past fifteen years," he said, "we have referred for treatment or detoxification or employment or for housing or for any need that the drug user or the former drug user may have, some 42,000 people. We have made surveys in the community, and we know that in Harlem alone, we have over 150,000 hard-core addicts. We know that in the city of New York, we have more than a half-million hard-core addicts roaming the streets. Just out there existing. It's a struggle for survival. We know that these people are receiving drugs every day, and despite what the government says—federal, state and local—they are not doing the job that they *can* do to halt the smuggling of drugs into this country."

Throughout his years as an activist minister, Dempsey continued to go to school. "I went to Brooklyn College at night for a number of years and started my education. It was interrupted, but I continued to study whenever I had a chance." He calls himself an "outside preacher." "Rather than the old line of spiritual minister who does nothing but preach and conduct prayer meetings, and who stays inside, I'm an outside preacher. My work is social action." And his formal education has followed that line. He feels that his years of experience as a social-action minister have complemented his formal training.

"After many years," he continued, "I went back and did my undergraduate work in the School of Education and also in the School of Continuing Education at N.Y.U. I spent four years to get the A.A. degree, and then I went back—I went to the School of Ed, preprofessional social work for the B.S. degree. And now, I'm working on the M.S.W. in the Graduate School of Social Work at N.Y.U.

"But the thing that has helped me more, especially in the education—after being out of school a long time—is that I was able to combine experience with education. And I'll tell you, I've never seen anything like it, because it did something to me. It helped me so much. And from what I learned from the instructors and from students, that they were greatly helped by my participation and what contribution that I was able to make during class discussions and in other areas where we did have problems in the school, as you know. Social problems."

Reverend Dempsey's educational experience is quite different from that of Father Clark, coming out of a Catholic seminary in Michigan. Father Clark came from a Baptist family, but he was introduced to Catholicism as a teenager. He stated that he was impressed by "the aesthetic experience of getting into that whole mystical thing, you know, with incense and Gregorian chant and dimly lit churches and—just a whole beautiful thing." He also acknowledged that joining the Catholic Church was a kind of logical step toward entering an integrated society. "I think that this was really just another step, because the church was so white. And to become a Catholic was really to have made it."

After Clark's seminary training, the bishop told him he was being assigned to an all-white parish in Ypsilanti. The bishop said: "We have chosen this place, Father, because we think it will be most consistent with your training and with your temperament."

Clark later declared: "I didn't appreciate the full meaning of what he had said to me until after I had been there for about three years. And then it began to dawn on me what he had really said was that, if that was consistent with

my training and my temperament, my training had prepared me to be more white than black."

At first, Father Clark felt he was a good priest, trained
well to serve the needs of his parishioners. He also believed
that "when I went to Ypsilanti, it seemed to me that my
job was to convince people that I was as good as any white
priest who had ever served in any parish." It was during
his four years in Ypsilanti that he began to rethink his role
as a black priest. This was after the mid-1960's, in the years
of the development of Black Power, black consciousness,
and it was then that Clark began to perceive himself as
the Malcolm X of the Roman Catholic Church.

But he had not reckoned with either his own personality
or the inadequacies of his training for such a role. A young
black priest trained in a white Catholic seminary simply
does not have the same formal or informal training of a
Malcolm X trained on the streets of Harlem and in the
prisons. Clark stated that he came to realize this after some
months of agony in trying to adjust to a black life-style.

The black parish to which he was assigned needed skills
he did not possess. It needed the skills of a Reverend
Dempsey. Declared Father Clark: "It was a parish, in my
opinion, which needed a great deal of social activity on the
part of the priests. And I really feel that somebody with
fewer hang-ups or with fewer reservations could have been
most effective. But what I really think they needed was
someone trained in the field or interested in the field of
community organization. They were trying to get together
enough of the talent in that area to begin to bring some
kind of creative pressure to bear on the problems that they
had. And it seemed to me that to enthrone a rectory priest
in that situation was just a terrible mistake. People didn't
come for that. They came either for basic social needs, like
they were having financial problems or they needed a job
or they had someone who was sick and they didn't know

how to get in touch with the medical resources, or they were strung out on dope and needed somebody either to help them get into a program or whatever services you could provide along that line. Or they needed a community organizer who would be able to work with people in the community, to get something going. But they didn't need me."

Father Clark worried about his relationship to the black community and to the black struggle. He thought that all black Catholics had an identity problem in this regard, because they had been socialized into a different—a white—world. He was not happy about this, but he was groping for answers to the problem. It meant, in the strongest terms, that he had to overcome much of his earlier training, training that found him more prepared, as the bishop concluded, to serve an all-white parish in Ypsilanti than to serve an all-black parish in inner-city Detroit.

He summed up his thoughts in the following manner: "I don't think that black people have had the same type relationship either to the black movement or really to black culture, once they become Roman Catholics. I know for myself when I look at my relationship with a thought to the contemporary black movement, I don't really see myself in terms of black ministers or black preachers. Because I think that to a large extent I work for an institution which does not touch the lives of large numbers of blacks, and therefore doesn't concern itself with the same questions or situations that others would. I think to some extent we struggle to change that. *I still think that my training has prepared me to be really a black servant in a white household.* And I think that black servants in white households tend to come at the whole black thing from a different point of view.

"We spend so much of our time trying to rediscover our black roots. And I just don't know whether a minister who has spent his whole life in a black community working with black people goes through the same type of problems. Even if he's attempting some kind of role redefinition, I don't know if he has to go through the same things we go through."

The experiences of Reverend Lewis in Winston-Salem and Reverend Dempsey in Harlem tend to confirm Father Clark's tentative conclusions. Although Lewis went off to all-white Andover-Newton in Boston, there never seemed to be any doubt that he would be preparing himself to serve an essentially black congregation. And if he had any different thoughts about what the nature of that service would be, he had a grandfather and probably many others there in the black community to remind him otherwise. Lewis, in fact, found his experiences in the seminary to be "fascinating." "Sort of an uplift type of thing. Mountain-top type experience in a way—especially for a young kid who had not been exposed to the world too much and who had not been away from home."

On the other hand, Reverend Dempsey had been in and out of the Army in World War II. He began his ministerial career expecting to work with young black people on crucial community problems, and he seemingly brought as much in the way of day-to-day experiences to his formal training as he received.

Neither Lewis nor Dempsey felt their formal training to be irrelevant to their pastoral work—quite the contrary. Like Reverend Haygood in Tuskegee, they had always assumed that they would serve an all-black constituency. Thus they could take from their formal training those aspects which were relevant and useful, and consciously or unconsciously reject the rest.

It is interesting to note, in this connection, the experiences of Father Lorentho Wooden. He attended a black college, Morehouse College, in Atlanta, at the same time that Martin Luther King, Jr., was a student there. While at Morehouse, Wooden took a few religion courses and "dug all the good preaching," but he did not finally decide on going to seminary until he graduated and had spent a year "messing around, waiting tables in Atlanta." He won a scholarship to the University of Chicago, and through his contacts with a professor there, he became acquainted with the Episcopal Church. He was impressed by "some beautiful liturgical services." His political, social and religious ideas were undergoing reexamination. He became associated with a white liberal-left group at the University, and his ideas on racial integration and religion were forming.

"I was still at that time African Methodist Episcopal and on a strong integration kick," he recalled. "So that I was beginning to question then the possibility of ever working out the reconciliation of Christ in a church that by its very name was separatist. This was the way I saw it at that time. In other words, how could I ever reconcile men within the African Methodist Church? Why don't these people change the name of that church and begin to move? So I was beginning to become disaffected with the A.M.E.'s, plus the fact that some of the men were very jealous of guys like us who were beginning to get an education beyond their point.

"I remember a minister at Woodlawn A.M.E. [in Chicago] with whom I worked, and he was always knocking me, putting me down for getting an education and for going to the University of Chicago, that den of Communists, et cetera. He really turned me off.

"So I am, then, ready to make a move, both for integration purposes and for purposes of working out the reconciliation of Christ. And what would be better than to go into this beautiful, liturgical, education-oriented Episcopal Church?"

After returning South for a year or two without taking a degree ("I had a hang-up with exams and papers, et cetera, not unknown among young black guys leaping out of the South out of a different subculture into this whole highly competitive thing"), he enrolled in General Theological Seminary in New York. This turned out to be a frustrating, unhappy experience. "I'd gone through that whole Negro-radical thing at the University of Chicago. And to put me in this buttoned-down, Yale-Harvard, closed group was like taking me out of water. I was the most unhappy guy. I began to rebel. I wouldn't get a haircut, and this was in the days before the Afro, and you know what that meant. I felt my inferiority more intensely than at any other place."

He spent long hours walking the streets of Harlem. "I was losing my identity. I was on that integration kick, and here's what began to turn me. So I went to Harlem to remember who I was." He dropped out of school, got married, worked for a year or so in a neighborhood center in New Jersey and "was looking to get into somebody's school so I could get certified, because I'm nothing now." He finally spent two years at Episcopal Theological School in Cambridge, Massachusetts, and was then assigned to two black churches in Florida. Thus after three seminary schools (he never received a B.D. degree) and considerable reflection, he began to pastor and was associated with a black Episcopalian priest in Miami who was from the Bahamas. The wisdom he gained from this association must have been somewhat disconcerting, however.

"He taught me a lot of what I know in terms of a black ministry in the Episcopal Church," Wooden recalled. "The first lesson was that if you're going to pastor black people, you'd damn well better throw away the books you learned from in seminary and look at the people you're dealing with."

Wooden's formal training was only a beginning for him. He is now constantly reading and thinking out his relationship to his faith, his parishioners and society. He has not accepted all the tenets of the new Black Theology; his religious faith and training will not permit him to accept some of its major premises as he understands them.

"I've had a whole experience with that—in that civil-rights thing and that whole black revolution. Man, that is dangerous, very dangerous. I was consumed by a passion. And within that I understood what Paul said: 'We fight not against flesh and blood, but against principalities and powers and the rulers of the darkness of this world.' Because that thing of blackness is a power. That thing—you know.

"Like what Elijah Muhammad [leader of the Black Muslims] is saying, that 'Black men are God.' And that's what my religion ultimately sets itself against. Against the rulers of the darkness of this world.

"In other words, we are, like, so involved in a power struggle here and now between who's going to dominate what we've got here that we forget that we all, we *all* belong somewhere else, really. We didn't put ourselves here. That's the way I would say it. And that power, that very attractive, fascinating power, to subsume men completely in this kind of an enterprise is what Paul understood to be the power of this world. Not just a Cadillac and the money and the prestige and all. But the love of it, you know, that really makes you spiritually become a priest of that whole way of life. And I think the black thing is like that.

"This, incidentally, is my criticism of [James] Cone. It's forming slowly. As if blackness was God. I mean, it's *irrelevant,* and you forget that it's just a tactic. It's like a game. If a guy is moving out here in a racist way and you want to checkmate him, and so you make a counterracist move.

You understand me? And you get so good at the game that you forget it *is* a game. That whether it is black or white is *irrelevant* really to being human. Well, irrelevant is a strong term, but say something less than what we call under the aspect of eternity."

Ultimately, unlike Father Clark, Father Wooden does not feel himself to be a black servant in a white household. But, like Clark, he did have difficulty at times in reaching his congregation. Whether this was the result of a weakness in his formal training that did not prepare him to deal with the kind of parishioners he had to pastor or whether it was some defect in his own style cannot be answered. Father Wooden had considerably more experience working with community groups (the narcotics program in Harlem, the antipoverty agency in New Rochelle, neighborhood centers) than Clark, and this undoubtedly has helped him immeasurably, as it has Reverend Dempsey, in applying his formal theological training and dealing with his church. It has given him a confidence in his views and in his role that is not evident with Father Clark. In addition, only Clark, of those interviewed at length, served for a period in an all-white parish. The others knew fairly well from the outset that they would be pastoring black churches, and this fact could well have played a part in making them more resistant to the more obviously non-black-culture oriented parts of their formal training.

This is not an unknown phenomenon with some black college students, especially. Overtly or covertly, they reject those aspects of their formal training they know to be clearly irrelevant to the culture from which they came and to the community to which most of them will return. And if those students are to be black preachers, this talent for selectivity is an absolute necessity.

IX

Self-Reliant Individualists

After talking to a wide variety of black preachers and studying their careers, one receives the clear picture that many of these men are quite self-reliant, and in many ways self-made individualists—even those who speak and act in terms of the need for collective, united action in the black community. This is particularly true in the rather autonomous, independent black churches, but it is also found among those black ministers in white denominations in which the particular church is part of a larger, more centralized structure.

This characteristic probably stems from the fact that these men realize that they must be, in a real sense, entrepreneurs. They must marshal their personal talents to build and maintain a congregation. In most instances, they receive virtually no financial support from an ecclesiastical hierarchy. So they are required to rely on whatever resources they can mobilize personally. In large measure their success in attracting parishioners depends, and they know this, on their personal magnetism. Their livelihood derives greatly from that collection plate on Sunday and from periodic fund drives. If the members give and give generously, the church and the preacher prosper. If collections are substantially small, then the preacher knows he must do something to increase them or look for other ways to supplement his income.

The art, and it is precisely that, of raising money at black mass meetings is a highly developed one, and frequently black preachers are called upon to perform this function. The techniques vary from having people walk down front to make their contribution to "raising money in rounds": first the ten-dollar bills, next the fives, then the ones. Some preachers make a game of this, combining wit and wisdom with out-and-out cajolery. In some large churches, preachers spur competition by having various clubs within the church compete. In one Northern church of approximately nine hundred members, there are clubs of the various "home states" from which the members migrated: South Carolina, North Carolina, Virginia, Georgia. "I play on their pride," the minister said. "I tell them that I know the folks from such-and-such state are not going to be outdone by so-and-so state. That they want people to know that they've made it up North and support their church. And we put a big poster in the lobby, you see, showing the amount each week. Folks got a lot of pride, you know. And there's always this little friendly rivalry between where you came from. And I play on this."

Many black preachers of small churches expect to have to supplement their incomes. Reverend Wooden described himself as a "hustler," meaning, of course, that if the members "don't pay me enough money, what do I do? I get myself an additional job." And he went into Harlem and became an administrator for a dope-addiction agency for two years, "serving as a therapist and hustling money and hiring and firing people and going into prisons, et cetera. This was my nine-to-five job, and in the evenings I had my meetings with the church and did whatever I needed to do in New Rochelle. Weekends, I was a priest. I did my callings on Saturday, necessary callings. . . . It worked all right, but it killed me. It meant that I had top responsibility for two institutions. I had to worry about two things."

This was not the first time Wooden had to manage two establishments. When he left the seminary in Cambridge, he was given two small churches to pastor in Florida. Both were small and financially poor, and both required a great deal of leadership and work. "I was not given one, but two churches. *And I had to get it!* No other way of saying it." In the two years he was there, he acquired land for one of the churches to build on, increased the membership of the other, and built a house for his family. ("They put us in a broken-down shack, and I promised my wife that if she'd just stick with me, I'd build her a house. And I did, a ten-thousand-five-hundred-dollar house.")

Wooden's experiences are not uncommon to many black preachers, and some, like Reverend Lewis in Winston-Salem, specifically try not to have to rely on the church for their livelihood. They know that many churches are very poor, and it is a serious strain on church finances to try to support the minister and his family comfortably. Reverend Lewis deliberately sought a situation where his other occupation would make him independent of the church for a livelihood. His church, Mount Pleasant Baptist, pays him a small salary, but his primary income is derived from his full-time position on the faculty of the State University.

"For one thing," he said, "I've seen it look too mercenary. I've seen situations where the minister has to think of techniques and all kinds of things to raise money. And then I've seen a good portion of that money go to him. I mean, I don't object to that particularly, but I grew up* in the church, and I recognize the financial limitations of many of the members, because of the kinds of jobs that they have. They just don't have overwhelming amounts of money.

"And I feel that to be already, myself, somewhat, quote, established, to be in a position, a job where I can support my family and live comfortably as I want, and then to give my services, then I feel like it's not a matter of do or die, it's a matter of do because it's something you really love to do and enjoy doing."

Again, the dual responsibility requires tremendous energy and self-reliance, but most ministers to whom I talked took this in stride. Only a few who had to seek supplementary employment bemoaned the necessity for this, accusing black church members of not financially supporting the church and the minister as much as possible.

But with many ministers there is a strong sense of personal pride as they tell how they have struggled to educate themselves, build their churches, engage in community activity and provide for their families. The ethic of work and achievement is strong with many of them: If you work hard, you can achieve.

Reverend Dempsey in Harlem tells proudly how he went to school for years, constantly worked against the narcotics rackets and educated his children. "All of these things have been done in the past few years," he said. "It's not an easy task, but it says something. That if you really want to do something, you can."

Some ministers, like Reverend Haygood, will pronounce that they believe in the "free-enterprise system," even while they advocate extensive social-welfare programs. And this belief is closely tied to a strong spiritual commitment not too unlike the Calvinist belief in the relationship between Christianity and prosperity. Haygood is fond of citing millionaires who received their inspiration from religion.

"You know H. Ross Perot, now in Dallas, Texas, a billionaire?" he asked. "He was attending the Highland Park Presbyterian Church, which is our largest Southern Presbyterian Church. This is in Dallas, Texas, and incidentally I've had the opportunity of preaching there at this church to the women of the church. But anyway, H. Ross Perot was attending service on one Sunday morning. During the time that Dr. William Elliott, the pastor, was talking, the idea for this invention that he came up with came to him and at some time last year, he was pointed out by *Time* magazine as being one of our new billionaires. Well, now, this man was spiritually motivated. The idea within the confines of the sanctuary came to him, you see."

Undoubtedly, an evangelist like the Reverend Frederick Eikerenkoetter, better known as "Reverend Ike," is one of the most prominent exponents of the doctrines of self-reliance and individualism. Reverend Ike has a radio program heard in twenty-eight states and in approximately sixty-five cities from coast to coast throughout the week. At thirty-five years of age, he has churches in New York and in Los Angeles, and the services are attended by thousands. The churches have several Rolls-Royce limousines, and Reverend Ike has a very large home in Rye, New York, on Long Island Sound—an exceedingly wealthy neighborhood.

"My bag is really dealing with people on an individual level," he said. "I believe that the reason for problems which we have in society begin within the individual. And very frankly, to tell you the truth, my religion or my gospel is positive self-identity. To get each person to believe in the divinity, or the dignity within himself."

He reminded his listeners that he had a difficult, poverty-stricken childhood, and that he committed himself, personally, to overcoming that background by relying on his own efforts, not by receiving welfare or "handouts." He continued: "Coming out of the background such as I did where my mother taught school, seven grades in one room, and where I and my mother walked to school four miles a day and four miles back, and where I've experienced a degree of poverty equal perhaps to anybody who has any problems, I don't believe that anybody can give you anything. And I personally don't believe in welfare. I am against it. And I even speak against it here [in his church].

"So, in a sense, to tell you the truth, I really don't represent the bag that most of the Negro preachers are going after now. I just don't. I do not think—as I said out here once, I believe welfare has its place, but don't make it a resting place. No one has a right to be a parasite. And my business is trying to teach these people, 'Listen, don't accept any labels of self-identity from Washington or from the politicians. Don't let anybody tell you you're underprivileged. Believe in yourself and you can make your own way.' And that is where I am. And I'm not interested in race at all."

This attitude of individual self-reliance held by Reverend Ike extends to racial matters. He is not an advocate of Black Power or black nationalism, and he chuckled when he related the following incident: "I usually say, when I'm receiving an offering on a weekend when I only have one service, that the only color we believe in here is green—green power.

"And I usually tell about the other day when I was riding along one of the big boulevards there in Los Angeles. And the driver was driving me in one of the official Rolls-Royce limousines which the church has. And there was a black boy hitchhiking. He saw me pass by, sitting in the back of the limo, and he raised his fist in the black salute. We pulled up to the light, and about that time, he had caught up with us. And I said to my chauffeur, 'I can't resist this.' I let the window down and stuck my head out, and I yelled, 'This isn't Black Power, baby, this is Green Power.'

"So very frankly, in the religious, political, black scene,

I don't fit. I'm not interested in having pull with the mayor or with the governor—at all. I'm interested in teaching each person his own dignity, his own capability, his own possibility. And I believe that *every person makes his own way*."

There is, of course, a vast difference between the individual self-reliance of Wooden, Dempsey, Haygood and Lewis on the one hand, and that of Reverend Ike on the other. The former are willing to transform that individualism into collective action, and, in fact, would conclude that only by doing so will conditions be changed for large numbers of people. Reverend Ike is not of that school of thought. On the spectrum of political opinion from left to right, he would be considered the most conservative of the ministers interviewed. The other men believe there are limits to what an individual can do by and for himself in a mass, industrialized society. Among a young, activist-minded group, Reverend Ike is considered irrelevant, a detriment to the community or both. His appearance, riding in a Rolls-Royce, very handsomely and modernly dressed, causes some critics to accuse the ministry of preying on a vulnerable congregation and misleading them to believe that their lowly condition is a result of their own failures and inabilities to improve themselves.

In spite of these blatant differences, it is very difficult to find black preachers who will openly criticize the style and action of a person like Reverend Ike. There is no lack of criticism from laymen, but it is an entirely different story with preachers.

As with many businessmen, it is as if the ethic of individualism is so strong that it permits them to be quite tolerant of their colleagues. This is especially the case as long as their own individual endeavors are not harmed by the acts of others in the profession. Although it is not usually stated in this way, in a sense the black preachers *are* businessmen engaged in one of the largest industries in the black community—religion. Most of them, of course, would understandably reject this label. But they must build a congregation—customers, clients, patients—and show a profit, both pecuniary and psychological. In addition, they must, in some instances, actually manage vast properties. And it is known, obviously, that except in the most flagrant cases of abuse, businessmen of whatever kind are not too openly critical of one another. Highly competitive, of course, but not censorious of one another's character or philosophy. If anything, like businessmen in other industries, they are more prone to *admire* (and in some instances, envy) the success of fellow ministers, notwithstanding the methods used to achieve that success.

I do not know one black preacher to whom I talked who would readily and openly agree with this analysis and conclusion. But the assessment, I feel, is valid nonetheless. In many ways they must be sensitive to the marketplace; they must display their wares in the best possible light; they must, as Wooden says, be "hustlers" in the best meaning of that term. In many ways they must be superb salesmen who know how to package and sell themselves before they can get their "customers" to buy *their* particular product. This product is not so much a general religious faith, but *their* particular enunciation of that faith.

X

Youth, the Ministry and the Church

There is a widespread attitude among many young black people in their late teens through their twenties and mid-thirties that the church, generally, is not a very useful institution in the black community. Their criticisms are even more severe against ministers. When they have kind words for a minister, these are usually directed at his role as a community activist, not as a preacher per se. By "not a very useful institution," they usually mean that the church serves as a major pacifier of masses of people. This criticism sees the church as playing the role of making people complacent with their lot on earth and offering them rewards in the hereafter. The ministers are seen as the major perpetrators of this belief, as well as the major beneficiaries. The young critics see the ministers in relatively comfortable homes, driving big cars and living off the hard-earned money of the poor parishioners. And in some cases, even when the church and the minister are involved in social-welfare projects, some younger people will voice an opinion typified by the following comment of a black college student: "They wouldn't be doing even those things if it didn't mean something in their pockets for them personally."

Reverend Lewis in Winston-Salem described the response of one young college student: "Although one young man admitted that at one time he had thought of the ministry as a profession . . . then he decided he didn't want to do it. The reason he gave was that he thought there was a lot of hypocrisy among the clergy. Because he saw people who preached to the people on Sunday and they rode off in Cadillacs on Monday."

The accusation of hypocrisy runs throughout the discussions by both youth and ministers about attitudes toward the church and preachers. Reverend Haygood in Tuskegee, Alabama, made the following observation: "I see the young people of today really being more religious than their elders. The young people today are looking for a contagious sense of authenticity. They're looking for that which is real and for that which has meaning. And they're totally disillusioned by the hypocrisy of their parents. Now, they want to make religion relevant in their everyday lives. And they cannot understand when their parents tell them to do one thing, and, behold, they see their parents involved in another. They like sooth; they don't like deception, and they're willing to face the truth.

"I don't think the young people are turning away from the church; I think they are turning away from the institutionalized church as we have known it—the traditional church, as we would call it. That is, that church that doesn't have anything to say about healing the man who is sick, about ministering to the man who is mentally ill, and a church that doesn't have anything to say about relieving the oppressed from oppression, and about giving a sense of consolation to those who are in prison. I think that this kind of church is totally irrelevant to our today's youth."

Haygood sees the young people in the vanguard of a growing spiritual revolution in the country, one that is deeply religious, but not in the traditional sense. And this, too, is a prevalent theme in these discussions. Haygood says:

"We have the Jesus movement going on among our young people today. And they are saying—they're getting off the drugs, and they are saying that Jesus is a good high. Well, this spiritual movement is pretty much in effect throughout the whole country today. People turning—we're on the threshold of one of the most powerful spiritual revolutions that we've had in a long, long time in this country. It may be growing out of the fear, out of the frustration, out of the uncertainty of America itself. It could be growing out of a great despair and great despondency, but people are turning back to religion. It's not the traditional religion."

This movement to which Haygood refers has not been espcially evident among black youth, college or noncollege. To the extent that it exists, it appears to be largely a white, middle-class-youth phenomenon. Black youth, in some instances, may be turning back to the church, but not for spiritual reasons. Rather, what one finds in some cases is black youth looking to the church, not to religion, as a potential institution for revived social action.

Father Clark in Detroit is not optimistic about a possible working relationship between the young and adults. His experiences thus far in his parish point largely to rejection of the adults by the youth. He observed:

"What I find among the young black people in this parish, this neighborhood, is they don't want any adults messing around in their thing. So they will organize something down at the high school, and interested ministers from the community will say, 'What can we do to help?' And they just say, 'Stay our of our way, man.' They're very secretive; they don't want us to participate in the program."

Therefore, Clark suspects, the best thing adults can do under the circumstances is to organize on their own and perform a kind of "auxiliary role." By this he means that perhaps the adults can go to the principal and teachers and talk to them about the problems in the school. In this way the adult group will not be linking up directly with the youth, but rather they will be working in the same direction in parallel organizations.

Father Wooden has similar observations to make about the lack of attractiveness of the church to the young people:

"You cannot outweigh fourteen to fifteen to sixteen years of a cynical relationship to an institution as this young generation has had. I think it is a fair statement that the young generation is pretty much turned off of the old-time religion. That's where they see it. Their last memory is the Sunday school. And that memory is a bunch of goody-goody ladies and old men who are doing something, but they don't know what. But it doesn't cut any ice with the real world they know.

"So, I'm not getting them. They're not coming around. I marry them. I baptize their children. They love to have me around. I look good. I can talk, but they don't really support the institution."

Some ministers, however, have not found working with young people to be a particularly vexing problem. This, again, may very well be a result of the fact that they have had such a relationship over an extended period of time. Reverend Dempsey in Harlem is a good example. As noted earlier, he started out over twenty years ago focusing on youth work. In Brooklyn, he was chairman of the Youth Work Committee and first vice-president to the Senior Youth Council of the local NAACP. Operating then out of the Cornerstone Baptist Church in Brooklyn, he helped organize "in that church the first youth movement in the State of New York." Moving to Adam Clayton Powell's church in Harlem in the mid-1950's, he was director of the boys' club there, a position which involved him in virtually all the problems of a lower-class, depressed-inner-city youth culture—housing, crime, narcotics, unemployment.

Now, in his own church on 125th Street in Harlem, in the middle of one of the worst narcotics areas in the city, he works very closely with youth. On the top floor of his church is the Dempsey House of Hope, which serves as a kind of haven for destitute narcotics addicts. It is a referral center "and a sort of rehabilitation center for drug users who go through detoxification or who kick the habit and who need some further help that the city and federal government have refused to give to those people." Dempsey and his church also have a training program during the summer in conjunction with the New York State Division for Youth.

His involvement with youth has led to an assorted number of activities. He describes his attitude in this way:

"Wherever the action is, that's where I try to be. Last night I had to serve as a judge for a hot-pants contest at the Audubon Ballroom, 'cause some of our young people were involved. And the people, they wanted me to be there. And the young people, they would not take 'No.' So I went. Because, first of all, this is the way I look at it. These young people are trying to do something. They're trying to accomplish something. Well, whereas I might not be personally interested in, let's say, dancing—I have nothing against dancing—but then, again, for their sake, as long as something is nice, as long as it's helpful and healthy, I see no reason why I shouldn't encourage the young people, and try to understand their side of the problem. And they, in turn, will be able to make their own decisions —if not now, later on, I think, in a more intelligent way than they would if I were to stand back with some sort of negative approach and say Don't do this, and Don't do that."

Another matter of much concern to many ministers is the number of black students attending theological schools. Today there are 808 black students in theological schools. Of that number, thirty-two are reported in Roman Catholic schools and 776 in Protestant or nondenominational schools. This latter figure represents an increase of 111 from the spring of 1970. The largest number of black students today are enrolled in schools in the Southeast and the East, and 544 are enrolled in predominantly white institutions of intermediate size (151–300). The largest number of black students enrolled in denominational schools are in American Baptist, United Methodist and United Presbyterian seminaries.

Reverend Lewis states that the relatively low salaries ministers receive is a major deterrent to many young people's entering the profession.

One black religious group that insists that it is not having too much difficulty recruiting youth is the Nation of Islam—better known as the Black Muslims. As mentioned in Chapter III, there are no reliable figures on the size of this organization, but one is able to observe its impact on sizable mass gatherings and to observe the overt manifestations of its growth: businesses, farms, and so on.

There is little question that more than a few young black people have been attracted to the organization in the last few years—not for religious reasons, but for political reasons. And these youth are college as well as noncollege people. Out of the intense, highly emotional atmosphere of Black Power and black consciousness of the late 1960's, there developed a proliferation of groups and ideologies. But very few of these were able to point to tangible programs and successful projects in the early 1970's. Not so with the Black Muslims. At the National Conference of All-African Peoples in Atlanta in 1970, covering a broad range of the black political spectrum, a minister of the Nation of Islam admonished his listeners that the Nation of Islam *was* acquiring land, *was* developing black businesses, schools, farms. The message was clear: The Black Muslims were not just talking; they were performing. This, and similar pronouncements, made a profound impression on the essentially young, nationalist-inclined black audience. One black college student later said: "I'm not a Muslim—yet. But you've got to admit that those people are putting it together."

Many young blacks are also impressed with the seemingly smooth functioning of the group, and with the lack of ideological confusion within its ranks. The Muslims are very clear in what they believe and what they want. Many young black activists have suffered through interminable internal ideological and leadership fights in other black organizations, and they have seen some of their previously well-respected organizations develop and disintegrate. But this has not been the case with the Black Muslims. They have survived, and they have not "gone over to the white man." Unlike the Black Panthers, the Muslims have not been deterred in their programs by protracted, violent struggles with the law-enforcement authorities. While young black people do not by any means sanction the actions of the police against the Black Panthers, many definitely saw the party on a no-win collision course with the State.

The Black Muslims use bravado in their rhetoric, but they also know how far to go. And they busily emphasize and implement black economic unity and development, as well as black pride and black self-respect.

A decade ago, some observers of the Muslim movement

were saying that the group attracted people largely in the lower socioeconomic category. That is probably still the case. But one hears today much more sympathetic comments coming from educated blacks and from those in middle-income brackets. Again, these expressions of sympathy are clearly not related to an affinity for the religious teachings, but to the racial and economic achievements. In fact, many black college students have stated that they could easily join the organization were it not for the stringent religious requirements. But this, of course, is precisely a major tenet of the group and probably a major reason for its survival. Those persons who join and become solid members have been religiously converted. One of the major demands of the group is to have the United States government give a sizable piece of land to blacks to rule as a sovereign entity. Very many black people see this as absolutely unrealistic, politically. But at the same time, this separatist aspect of the program is less a deterrent than some of the personal religious requirements.

I mentioned this hesitancy on the part of some young blacks in a discussion with a Muslim minister, indicating that some had stated that they saw no reason to give up smoking or eating pork. The minister replied: "Then they're not ready, are they? But the time will come when they, like all black people, will see the truth of the teachings of the Honorable Elijah Muhammad. And they will follow him—gladly."

One need not debate this here. What is known, however, is that many young black people are looking for organizations that have not only rhetoric but viable programs. They want to involve themselves with groups that are actively engaged in doing constructive things for masses of blacks. I do not see them returning to the traditional church of their parents for religious reasons, but some are looking to those churches for sociopolitical action. The old rituals and symbols do not impress them. One might speculate that to the extent that any black religious group—Muslim, Methodist, Baptist or whatever —minimizes the mystical and stresses the practical, to that extent will it have a greater chance of recruiting younger people. Whether a Black Muslim appeal or a black Christian appeal is able to do this remains to be seen.

XI

Summary

While talking to a number of black preachers in the course of gathering material for this book, I was constantly struck by the number of ministers who cautioned me, "Now, I hope you're not going to be too hard on us"; or, "You've got to keep an open mind. We're not all bad, you know." There was a widespread defensive attitude about the profession. This was more frequently displayed by either the younger, more activist ministers or the middle-aged preachers who, while not very involved politically, spent much of their time trying to build their churches as active religious centers in the black communities. Usually, the older ministers did not particularly care what my attitude or orientation happened to be, on the apparent assumption that the image of their profession could be neither helped nor harmed thereby. Younger ministers tended to be concerned that I understood that there was a "new breed" of black minister coming on the scene, one who was more involved in the community problems of the parishioners and less concerned with personal, material wealth. Older preachers appeared more interested in discussing religious lessons in the Bible than in talking about civic or political matters. But more than a few of both types at first assumed, without any prior knowledge, that I was generally antagonistic toward their profession. They believed, in other words, that I had come to criticize and to find fault. This accounted for their defensive attitude. When I discussed this with several of them, they stated that their experiences had been generally negative with researchers, who usually had their own preconceived notions about what roles the ministers and churches ought to be playing.

The black preachers are accustomed to criticism, which many feel is based on generalizing from a "few bad apples in the barrel." They are used to being associated with either the jackleg preacher who is flamboyant and untrained or with Martin Luther King, Jr. They want to avoid being classed with the former, whom they consider undesirable and not at all representative. And they want to emphasize that the latter was an exceptional man who rose to heights unattainable by most people, clergymen or not. Therefore, they insist, it is unfair to measure all black ministers against Martin King.

Without question, black preachers cover the spectrum from pimps to paragons, riches to rags, radicals to reactionaries, scholars to charlatans. But there are some general characteristics that become manifest.

Those ministers in predominantly white denominations today appear to spend much more time than their black colleagues in the black Baptist, African Methodist and other black churches talking about their racial identity. They grapple constantly with "being black," and with the meaning that may have for a person, especially a clergyman, in a denomination in which all the literature, rituals, symbols, and most of the members are white. The preacher in a black denomination is less concerned with this problem, but frequently he will be involved in trying to "be relevant"—to make the church more meaningful in the lives of the black parishioners. As if, when Richard Allen, James Varick and the black Baptist ministers in the nineteenth century left the white denominations, that answered the question of racial identity. They know they are black people, but at times they are not quite sure what that calls for in developing specific church-related programs for the community. The new Black Theologians have provided one answer, the Nation of Islam another, but the search for relevancy continues.

This difference in outlook is illustrated by the experiences of a black Baptist preacher in Harlem, such as Reverend Dempsey, who saw a young dope addict die of an overdose of narcotics twenty-two years ago; and of a black Catholic priest in Detroit, like Father Clark, who was shocked by the abusive language of youngsters on a ghetto street. The former decided to devote his time to ridding the black community of the narcotics traffic; the latter, of necessity, had to spend his time becoming acculturated to an environment distinctly different from the one he had been prepared to serve.

The preachers in the black denominations do not spend as much time discussing preaching style and adapting their faith to the black parishioners. In a sense, the very existence of the separate black denominations is a function of an earlier, determined and successful effort to deal with those kinds of issues. Therefore, for many reasons, it is not surprising to find the most vocal and concentrated efforts toward reestablishing and redefining the meaning of a black identity among those black preachers in white denominations. In many cases, like Father Wooden and Father Clark, they left their childhood black church and deliberately sought a predominantly white church, in part for purposes of racial integration. It was Father Wooden who was impressed by the "education-oriented" Episcopal Church and who saw contradictions in, as he put it, the

African Methodist Episcopal Church, which by its very name was separatist. And it was he who had to escape to the streets of Harlem to attempt to rediscover his racial roots. It was Father Clark who saw his move out of the black Baptist church into the Catholic Church as a logical racial-integration move into the American mainstream. Later, he grew to doubt this and to begin to see that blacks had experiences and interests distinct from whites and that neither group had to or should apologize for these differences.

The black Baptist, A.M.E. and A.M.E. Zion preachers have understood all along the peculiar relationship of race to church. Granted, they react in many different ways. This is not to say, by any means, that they are more inclined to be black nationalists. Certainly this could not be said for men such as Richard Allen or Joseph H. Jackson. It is to assert, however, that they are more likely to find it easier to see a racial basis for their church's existence than the other black ministers, like Father Wooden in his earlier years at the University of Chicago. Even a black Baptist preacher who is not in any way a political activist, who spends his full time relating to a totally black congregation religiously, is less likely to raise questions of racial identity than a black Episcopalian priest like Father Wooden or a black Catholic priest like Father Clark.

Until recent years, this difference was interpreted as being between the "low" church and the "high" church. The former was considered more associated with lower socioeconomic classes, with a worship service that was highly emotional. The latter was middle class, quiet and restrained. And for the most part, it was the latter church that was considered more intelligent and more rational in its approach to religion. Today there is a reexamination of these kinds of conclusions. With the rise of black consciousness, scholars such as Professor Henry Mitchell and many black ministers are beginning to suggest that the style of worship found in the black denominations is one consistent with the culture of black people as a *racial* group, and not a function of socioeconomic class. This reexamination recognizes that the black preacher has always been not only a religious and political leader of his people, but also, and perhaps more importantly, a cultural leader.

He has always epitomized the major characteristics of his people. What they were, he reflected most. During slavery, the preacher was their major teacher. If they sought to revolt and protest, he was there to lead them and very often to inspire them. And the preacher has been the major indigenous leader to adapt whatever mood and movement of the black community to the cultural style of the people. This is what Reverend Andrew Young meant when he described the relationship among religion, the Southern black churches and the civil-rights movement in the 1950's and 1960's. The importance of the black preacher, then, has not been so much that he has been the primary innovator—although certainly he has been that—but that he has been the major figure to combine the movement of the masses with the cultural style of those masses. His value lies in his abilities as a *cultural* leader, more so than as a *political* leader.

This culture has been heavily religious in substance, and this has contributed to the preacher's authenticity. This characteristic may come to be shared, but it will not likely be preempted by other black leaders who have developed over the last few decades. The black lawyer, the black labor leader, the black community organizer, the black politician—all these people are growing in number in the black community. But until they develop pervasive, indigenous black organizational structures, they will have to rely heavily on the black preachers in those black churches for substantial help in reaching and mobilizing masses. This has been a major achievement of the NAACP; the church membership has been no small part of the support for that civil-rights organization. And a cursory survey of biographies of black ministers will show that very many have served on local NAACP boards. The religious orientation of the Black Muslims has served and sustained that organization. And this factor has been recognized by the young, militant Black Panther party. In May, 1971, Huey P. Newton declared:

> As far as the church is concerned, the Black Panther party, and other community groups who call themselves concerned with the political and not the spiritual, criticize the spiritual. We say that it's only a ritual; it's irrelevant, and therefore we have nothing to do with it. We say this in the context of the whole community having something to do with the church, usually on one level or another. That is one way of defecting from the community, and that is exactly what we did. Once we stepped outside of the thing that the community was involved in and said to them, "You follow our example; your reality is not true and you don't need it." I think that people do the thing that they think they need and they probably do it on that level, one way or another. . . .
>
> But until the people feel the same way I feel then I'll be rather arrogant to say dump the whole thing just as we were arrogant to say dump the church.

In describing the black preacher as a cultural leader, it is important to point out that this does not apply to that jackleg minister who, for all intents and purposes, is simply in the church as a commercial business. He is concerned essentially with making a living, with realizing as large a profit as possible, and he uses the prestige and position of the church and the pulpit to achieve this. He is a con man, a hustler, simplistic and banal, and a master of mass psychology. Only a romantic would contend that the jackleg preacher reflects any *viable* aspect of a culture. He preys on the lower-class, dependent community for his own ends. He uses people. He is willing, in much the same way as many businessmen, to represent himself and his services in any way that will maximize his income. There are more than a few of these black preachers around. Their response is an obvious one: They do not *make* people follow them. In other words, *caveat emptor*— let the buyer beware. These men operate above the law, and in that area just beyond the point of fraud.

To the people who follow them, these preachers are not frauds or con men. They are dynamic, insightful men of God. Probably the only way to eliminate this type of preacher is to change the socioeconomic conditions which create and sustain the core constituency on which he relies. As people improve themselves educationally and economically, they will demand a more thoughtful and involved ministry. It will be much more difficult for a minister simply to seduce and hustle his followers. But as long as many black people remain uneducated and trapped on the lowest levels of economic existence, the jackleg preacher will have a ready market in which to peddle his relatively simplistic and ignorant approach to life and religion. He will be able to provide simple answers to complicated issues. If, in fact, this *is* a reflection of a lower-class culture, it clearly is not a viable culture that provides the basis for a people to develop and deal with the problems of modern times. This kind of unintelligent approach might well serve to provide momentary comfort for a people; it might well provide them with psychological resources to survive. But more is needed than comfort

and survival if a people are to grow and become constructive contributors to modernity.

One important fact about the black preacher is that he
is essentially a *local* man. With the exception in modern
times of only a handful like Martin King, Joseph H. Jackson, Adam Powell and Malcolm X, the primary effectiveness of the black preacher is at the community, church
level. The attitude of the Reverend Henry Lewis of Winston-Salem is probably typical when he states that he prefers to concentrate on his local parish rather than at the
level of national convention. He feels the latter is more
preacher- than people-oriented in terms of developing relevant programs for the immediate church in the community. And Father Donald Clark's doubts at this time about
the efficacy of a certain kind of national organization of
black priests are probably valid. Such a national organization can serve as a spokesman, but little else. The preacher
is best, in whatever he does, when he is operating closest
to his people. His talents, skills and inclinations are there.
The more he progresses into the national arena—the halls
of Congress and the boardrooms of national corporations—
the less effective he is in combining his special skills as a
minister with the demands of activism. This is not to
suggest that he should not operate beyond the local level.
But when he does succeed it will probably not be his
peculiar ministerial talents that will sustain him, but
rather other acquired skills.

The more national his base, the more necessary it is to
develop many different styles and appeals. And most black
preachers frankly are not that versatile. A Martin Luther
King could do this, but he was, in fact, exceptional. A national organization could be much more effective in the
nonpolitical arenas, namely, in education and economic
ventures. The National Baptist Convention, U.S.A., has
a much greater chance of succeeding in its own educa-

tional programs and even in some forms of economic ventures than it has in attempting to influence national public policy by mobilizing a national, mass, black-church public. As long as the electoral political system is organized to respond to organized local constituencies, this limitation is not a particularly fatal one. That is, the best way the black churches can influence the Congress is not by passing resolutions in their national conventions, but by having the local churches in selected congressional districts organize their congregations to vote for or against specific candidates for Congress. The national convention can, on the other hand, proceed to develop and implement a quality educational program for the colleges under its jurisdiction. Or it can purchase land and start cooperative farming enterprises. These kinds of resources the national body *can* accumulate and develop, and in fact the task is probably best attacked at that level.

Another consideration is the fact that the black preacher must always spend considerably more energy in building and maintaining his local church. He has, at best, only a limited amount of time to devote to a national organization. Thus it is not surprising that some ministers would see the national organizations as essentially oligarchical in nature, run by the few without the continuous participation of the many. This is a universal characteristic, not peculiar to black ministers and churches.

How the black preacher involves himself locally is largely a matter of his own style and inclination. If he chooses to spend all his time tending his flock and maintaining his church, he is, for the present, probably on safe ground. He receives virtually no pressure from his congregation to become politically involved. For one thing, if he has a congregation many of whose members are politically motivated, they will find ways to express that interest outside of the church through labor unions, professional organizations, and so forth. They started out in the church for basically religious reasons. And most black congregations, essentially middle-aged and older, still make a distinction between the religious and the secular spheres. In such instances, the preacher can maintain his credibility as a church leader by tending to the business of the church. This will probably change, as will be noted later, as a new, younger group of people come on the scene. This is the essence of the comments of Father Wooden, Father Clark, Reverend Lewis, Reverend Haygood and Reverend Dempsey. And it is what Reverend Goodwin's church understands in putting together its various political and community-oriented programs. All these men are concerned that the church must change its focus if it is to attract and hold a younger crowd.

In the Reverend Kelly Goodwin's new five-hundred-thousand-dollar church in Winston-Salem, there are a number of programs aimed at young people as well as the black community at large. For several years the congregation held services in the gymnasium of a local YMCA following a fire which destroyed the old church building. Tediously, funds were raised to build a new structure. This was accomplished in 1969, the result being an ultra-modern, elaborate building with several classrooms, meeting rooms, up-to-date lighting, amplification and recording equipment and plush furnishings. Now Mt. Zion Baptist Church, under Reverend Goodwin's direction, engages in voter-registration drives and anti-narcotics, consumer education and recreational programs. The church newspaper carries articles on various social problems. Articles on drugs have included "The Pusher and His Source" and "Role of the Church Community in Combatting Drug Use." Announcements are printed of church members being elected presidents of local P.T.A.'s. One column in the church paper, the "Roving Reporters," asked people living in the vicinity: "In what areas of service can Mt. Zion be of help in improving the community?"

It is when the black minister chooses to become civically involved that one finds different reactions from the congregation now, ranging from quiet, subtle objection and noncooperation, as in Father Wooden's case, to strong, overt support as with Reverend Dempsey in Harlem or with the Philadelphia ministers during the years of "selective patronage." There is also the case of Reverend Haygood in Tuskegee, Alabama, who has to look outward to the national Presbyterian body for support and who only hopes that his local church does not present insurmountable obstacles to his work. (In April, 1972, he decided to give up his regular pastorate to assume full responsibility for Southern Vocational Christian College. He would continue to serve Westminster Presbyterian Church by visiting the sick and presiding at communion, and he would preach from time to time in other churches around the country. But it was clear that while he had received endorsement for the college from such interracial groups as The Church Women United of Alabama, he had not received full and wholehearted support from his own parishioners for his educational work outside the specific parish.) In such instances, it is necessary to make a distinction between the church and the preacher. Throughout this book, care has been taken to show the close ties between the two, but in these kinds of cases, clearly the preacher as an activist should not be confused with the church where the congregation does not support his outside activities.

One thing is clear, however, about the black preacher over the years: He has known how to survive with his people. He has known how fast and how far to take them, and this is largely because of his developed skills of leadership and his understanding of his followers. It has contributed to and is a result of his being a cultural leader. Most black preachers, in other words, would never have made the mistake the Black Panther party initially made and must now attempt to rectify. Father Wooden notes that he had "to step back a little in order to save the situation," meaning, apparently, to keep his church from developing an open schism over his role as an activist. And it is Reverend Goodwin in Winston-Salem who patiently brought his congregation along for years, holding services in an improvised gymnasium until they were financially able to build a big church structure. And from this base, the church members are able to reach out into the black community to begin to deal with other social problems.

Traditionally, the black preacher has been a master pacesetter. He has been able to develop for black people what the author John Oliver Killens calls "long-distance runners." He has been able to persist, and in the process, his people have been able to survive and persevere. This pacesetter role is related to the nature of the church as an improvised and adaptable black institution. But it is also a tribute to the skills of the preacher in the pulpit who has known when and where to push, when "to step back a little." At times, the preacher's patience has been interpreted as conservatism and a lack of drive or motivation. In fact, the way he acts frequently reflects his keen sense of timing and pace.

Unlike secular leaders, the preacher does not always have to respond to the moment and to the incident. He does not always have to react now, lest all be lost (notwithstanding Bishop Payne's fund-raising experiences in England after the Civil War). He can, in a phrase, "cool it," bide his time, fall back on the religious duties of his pulpit, wait for a more propitious moment and still have his flock with him.

Even in this, however, he must have a continuing sense of the times. It is very obvious that the societal demands of the last third of the twentieth century are fundamentally different from those one hundred, fifty or even twenty-five years ago. The aspirations of the black masses are moving ever upward and the black preacher must read this situation carefully. There is simultaneously a curious mixture in blacks of turning inward and looking outward. It is this new time which will challenge black leadership, including the preachers, in a way not previously experienced.

On balance, black preachers do indeed have a good track record of leadership; but tomorrow is never precisely like the day before, and precedent is valuable only up to a point. There is a basic question whether turning inward is the resurgence of communalism and black unity as evidenced by the new Black Theologians, or the intense self-reliant individualism of a Reverend Ike. It is neither possible nor practical to answer that question now. But the issues presented need not be confused. These are sharply divergent views, and at some point, one or the other will have to emerge dominant if the air is to be cleared. Reverend Ike preaches to his people to look to themselves as *individuals,* and he is not at all concerned with racial distinctions. The new Black Theologians advocate looking to themselves as a *group,* and racial identity is absolutely crucial.

In looking outward, there is a basic question whether this means looking to a viable Pan-Africanism, as evidenced by the statement of the Interreligious Foundation of Community Organizations, or eventual racial integration, when society no longer considers race relevant in public and religious policies. These are basic questions to be faced as American society moves toward the close of one century and the beginning of a new one.

Is it possible to reconcile the ideas of self-interested nationalism of Father Clark with the ideas of the eventual discovery of the "irrelevancy" (albeit "irrelevancy is a strong word") of race of Father Wooden?

There will always be the Reverend Dempseys fighting narcotics in Harlem, the Reverend Lewises developing religious-education programs in the Sunday schools, and the Reverend Haygoods teaching people job skills. And there will be the Reverend Dolls raising new questions in court about the relationship of Christians to one another.

Preachers are important cultural leaders. They will be intimately involved in raising the crucial questions and in helping others grope for the answers. They will be there to inspire, to relax, to cajole, to comfort, to motivate. They will preach their hearts out and eat all that chicken at Sunday dinners. They will visit the sick, and march, and sign petitions against South Africa. They will be there putting on those fund drives and building those big new shiny churches. And they will politick in those church conventions, and fuss and fight over money and women. What black people are, they are. Where blacks are going, they are going. And where they go, they will take their flock. They are dismissed by others only out of ignorance and arrogance. More of them will be politically inactive than politically involved. A new, younger, more insistent black generation will reject most of the former and keep a careful watch on the latter. And this means precisely that those who fail to measure up to the demands of a new day will be cast aside. Many are now, and have been for a long time, anachronisms in this society. And those men simply do not have a bright, popular future in the black community. If they fail to adapt to the requirements of a new time, they will, as Reverend Dempsey says, "miss the mark." They and their churches may linger for a time, even in some cases a long time, but they will not be relevant to the central thrust of social change.

In varied ways, the *modern* black preacher, despite his denomination and church, will have to develop those community-organization skills Father Clark worries about and Reverend Dempsey acquired through experience and formal education. The *modern* black preacher will have to act in the way Reverend Haygood insists the ministry must act, even if his particular project is disagreed with. The press of social change will make the strictly pulpit preacher irrelevant, as social forces and events eventually made the plantation slave preacher who preached obedience to the master irrelevant. His message and manners will simply be no longer useful.

It is very likely that ministers in the future will have to be trained in more than the lessons of the Bible. They will also need training in social work and economic and political skills. They will be called upon not only to visit hospitals and pray for the sick, but to attend school board meetings and join parents in protests. They will be expected to accompany delegations not only to national church conventions, but also to city council meetings. And the municipal planning board must become as familiar to the ministers as their own boards of deacons.

The preachers will not be expected to become jacks-of-all-trades. But an honest account will admit that there are too many today who are simply jacklegs, who have only a powerful set of lungs to recommend them. In the future the ministers must be able to bring more to their pulpits than a knowledge of the holy scriptures; they must begin to demonstrate, in a sense, a knowledge of the local statutes. And this is a need which will exist in the Southern rural communities as well as in the Northern urban cities. There is, in fact, a political awakening of blacks, led substantially by younger people who have come to maturity since the Korean War, and, indeed, since the 1960's. Whatever value the ministers served in an earlier time, the fact is that issues and needs have changed, and there is serious question whether black people can afford the luxury (if that is the word) of an institution and a leadership whose primary function is to serve as a haven from turmoil.

This is not to suggest that the ministers' duties as *religious* leaders will be diminished.

The preachers will be looked to for moral, ethical guidance, and an increasingly demanding and sensitive people

will probably not tolerate the loose standards characteristic of too many ministers today and in the past. Black
Americans are a people developing, coming out from
under a long period of subjugation and oppression. They
need rigor and talent and discipline and a value system
that contributes to unity and purpose and collective development—in this historical time and in this place. A
leadership, secular or religious, that overlooks this and
fails to respond, will be dysfunctional and will deserve to
be discarded.

A more socially concerned younger group will focus
more on the responsibilities of the minister in civic affairs
and as a moral, ethical force in this life, rather than as a
strict interpreter of religion who is largely concerned with
preparing for the life hereafter. Younger people will not
be frightened into heaven out of fear of burning in hell.
This group is not looking for saviors, but for solutions.
They are not looking so much for princes of peace as they
are for pioneers in protest. Many do not want a religion
that will pacify the people and render them meek and
humble, but one that will agitate and spur them to action.
They desire a Henry Highland Garnet, not a George Liele.

There will be, hopefully, very many (many more than
now exist) black preachers accepting these challenges, who
will be in those pulpits, out on those streets leading and
working with their people. To be sure, many have always
been there, and equally certain, they will be saddled with
those in their profession who will continue to shuck and
jive and hustle a vulnerable pew. This is unfortunate, but
unavoidable. By its very nature, the profession will inevitably attract the hustler. Only an intelligent, discriminating constituency will be able to separate the meaningful minister from the parasitic pimp, and render the latter
harmless. Hopefully, there will be many of those black
preachers in the future who will be preaching and protesting—and constantly looking for witnesses.

Source Notes

Chapter I

1. W. E. B. Du Bois, *Souls of Black Folk* (New York, Fawcett Publications, Inc., 1961), p. 141.
2. Carter G. Woodson, *The History of the Negro Church* (Washington, D.C., The Associated Publishers, 1921), p. 198.
3. See Edward Levine, *Irish and Irish Politicians* (South Bend, Indiana, University of Notre Dame Press, 1966).
4. Harry V. Richardson, "The Negro in American Religious Life," in *The American Negro Reference Book*, John P. Davis, ed. (Englewood Cliffs, New Jersey, Prentice-Hall, Inc., 1966), pp. 412–413.
5. Interviews conducted by the author, 1967–71.
6. See St. Clair Drake and Horace R. Cayton, *Black Metropolis*, Vol. II (New York, Harper & Row, Publishers, Harper Torchbooks, 1962).
7. Du Bois, *op. cit.,* p. 150.
8. Norman R. Yetman, ed., *Voices From Slavery* (New York, Holt, Rinehart and Winston, 1970), p. 95. Italics added.
9. Henry H. Mitchell, *Black Preaching* (New York, J. B. Lippincott Company, 1970), p. 47.
10. Benjamin Mays, *Born to Rebel* (New York, Charles Scribner's Sons, 1971), p. 140.
11. Woodson, *op. cit.,* pp. 258–259.
12. *Ibid.,* p. 75.
13. Charles Fager, *Uncertain Resurrection* (Grand Rapids, William B. Eerdmans Publishing Co., 1969), pp. 102–103.

14. *Ibid.,* p. 105.
15. Mitchell, *op. cit.,* p. 95.
16. Lerone Bennett, Jr., *Before the Mayflower* (Chicago, Johnson Publishing Co., 1961), p. 40.

Chapter II

1. Yetman, *op. cit.,* p. 13. Statement made by an ex-slave describing how some black preachers had to conduct services during slavery.
2. Quoted in Yetman, *op. cit.,* p. 335.
3. *Ibid.,* pp. 12–13.
4. *Ibid.,* p. 262.
5. A light-complexioned black man.
6. Yetman, *op. cit.,* p. 337.
7. *Ibid.,* pp. 182–183.
8. Woodson, *op. cit.,* p. 83.
9. Jupiter Hammon, *An Address to the Negroes in the State of New York by Jupiter Hammon, Servant of John Lloyd* (New York, Samuel Wood, 1806), p. 19.
10. Yetman, *op. cit.,* p. 308.
11. Benjamin E. Mays, *The Negro's God* (New York, Atheneum Publishers, 1968), pp. 19, 21.
12. Yetman, *op. cit.,* p. 13.
13. Woodson, *op. cit.,* p. 40.
14. *Ibid.*
15. The ironic fact that this was the same year and in the same city that the United States Constitution was drafted will not be lost on the student of American history.
16. Richard Allen, *The Life, Experience and Gospel Labors* (Philadelphia, Lee and Yokum, 1888), pp. 54–55.
17. John Hope Franklin, *From Slavery to Freedom* (New York, Alfred A. Knopf, 1963), p. 237.
18. Daniel A. Payne, *Recollections of Seventy Years* (New York, Arno Press and *The New York Times*, 1969), p. 28.
19. Daniel A. Payne, *History of the African Methodist Episcopal Church,* Vol. I (New York, Johnson Reprint Corporation, 1968), p. 277.
20. Payne, *Recollections,* p. 68.
21. Woodson, *op. cit.,* p. 67.
22. Gunnar Myrdal, *An American Dilemma* (New York, Harper & Brothers Publishers, 1944) , p. 696.

23. E. Franklin Frazier, *Race and Culture Contacts in the Modern World* (Boston, Beacon Press, 1957), p. 246.

24. Woodson, *op. cit.,* p. 66.

25. Mitchell, *op. cit.,* p. 76.

26. Mays, *The Negro's God,* p. 39.

27. Lerone Bennett, Jr., *Pioneers in Protest* (Baltimore, Penguin Books, Inc., 1969) , p. 50.

28. Payne, *Recollections,* pp. 100–101.

29. Woodson, *op. cit.,* p. 152. Professor Woodson states that the Reverend Charles Bennett Ray, for twenty years a Congregational minister in New York City, was better known for his work with the antislavery movement, the underground railroad, and as editor of *The Colored American* in the 1830's and 1840's.

30. Benjamin Quarles, *Black Abolitionists* (New York, Oxford University Press, 1969), p. 83.

31. Thomas R. Gray, ed., *The Confessions of Nat Turner, the leader of the late insurrection in Southampton (County) Va.* (Washington, D.C., The American Negro Monograph Co., 1910).

32. Woodson, *op. cit.,* p. 116.

33. Peter Williams, Jr., *An Oration on the Abolition of the Slave Trade; delivered in the African Church in the City of New York,* January 1, 1808 (New York, printed by Samuel Wood, 1808).

34. An address delivered on the celebration of the abolition of slavery in the State of New York, July 5, 1827, by Reverend Nathaniel Paul. Quoted in Herbert Aptheker, *A Documentary History of the Negro People in the United States* (New York, The Citadel Press, 1962), pp. 87–88.

35. Aptheker, *op. cit.,* p. 147.

36. *Ibid.,* p. 163.

37. Quarles, *op. cit.,* p. 68.

38. Franklin, *op. cit.,* p. 248.

39. John H. Bracey, August Meier and Elliott Rudwick, *Black Nationalism in America* (New York, The Bobbs-Merrill Co., Inc., 1970) , p. 40.

40. Quarles, *op. cit.,* p. 70.

41. Quoted in Quarles, *op. cit.,* p. 71.

42. Aptheker, *op. cit.,* pp. 205–206.

43. It is interesting to note that Frederick Douglass made a speech

several years later, in 1857, wherein he came closer to Garnet's position: "Power conceded nothing without demand. It never did and it never will. Find out just what any people will quietly submit to and you have found out the exact measure of injustice and wrong which will be imposed upon them, and *these will continue till they are resisted with either words or blow, or with both*" (italics added). The essence of Reverend Garnet's 1843 speech was precisely the same.

44. Bennett, *Pioneers in Protest,* p. 157.

Chapter III

1. Melville J. Herskovits, "Social History of the Negro," in Carl Murchison, *A Handbook of Social Psychology* (Worcester, Clark University, 1935), pp. 256–257.
2. E. Franklin Frazier, *The Negro in the United States* (New York, The Macmillan Company, 1949), pp. 16–17.
3. E. Franklin Frazier, *The Negro Church in America* (New York, Schocken Books, 1963), pp. 8–9.
4. Source: Richardson, *op. cit.,* p. 402.
5. Harry A. Ploski and Roscoe C. Brown, eds., *The Negro Almanac* (New York, Bellwether Publishing Co., Inc., 1967), p. 796.
6. The ten are: Albany; Alexandria; Amarillo; Atlanta; Austin; Baltimore; Baton Rouge; Belleville; Boston; Brooklyn.
7. A chart listed in Richardson, *op. cit.,* p. 411, shows that in 1960 there were approximately eight hundred "Negro priests." The source for this figure was Reverend J. B. Tennelly, S.S., of the Commission for Catholic Missions among the Colored People and the Indians, Washington. This figure is clearly incorrect. Father Donald Clark, in Part II, states that there are 170. Father Lawrence Lucas, president of the National Black Catholic Clergy Caucus and pastor of Resurrection Parish in Harlem, says there are more likely between 150 and 160.
8. Ira De A. Reid, "Let Us Prey!" *Opportunity* (September, 1926), pp. 274–278.
9. *Ibid.*
10. C. Eric Lincoln, *The Black Muslims in America* (Boston, Beacon Press, 1961), p. 4.
11. E. U. Essien-Udom, *Black Nationalism* (New York, Dell Publishing Co., Inc., 1962), p. 84.

12. Lincoln, *op. cit.,* p. 79.
13. Malcolm X, *The Autobiography of Malcolm X* (New York, Grove Press, Inc., 1966), p. 289.
14. *Ibid.,* p. 376.
15. *Ibid.,* pp. 338–339.
16. *Ibid.,* p. 340.

Chapter IV

1. Richardson, *op. cit.,* p. 412.
2. W. A. Daniel, *The Education of Negro Ministers* (New York, George H. Doran Co., 1925).
3. *Ibid.,* p. 14.
4. *Ibid.,* p. 15.
5. *Ibid.,* p. 41.
6. *Ibid.,* p. 95.
7. Charles Spencer Smith, *A History of the African Methodist Episcopal Church* (Philadelphia, Book Concern of the A.M.E. Church, 1922; New York, Johnson Reprint Corporation, 1968), p. 130.
8. *Ibid.,* pp. 295–296.
9. *Ibid.,* p. 233.
10. *Ibid.,* pp. 248–249.
11. A. W. Pegues, *Our Baptist Ministers and Schools* (New York, Johnson Reprint Corporation, 1970) , p. 618.
12. Owen Pelt and Ralph Lee Smith, *The Story of the National Baptists* (New York, Vintage Press, 1960), pp. 169–170.
13. "Five Million Baptists Plan Progress Drive," *Ebony* (December, 1964), p. 82.
14. Smith, *op. cit.,* p. 299.
15. Quoted in Smith, *op. cit.,* p. 75.
16. Peques, *op. cit.,* p. 563.
17. *Ibid.,* p. 576.
18. Reverend Charles Summer Long, *History of the A.M.E. Church in Florida* (Philadelphia, A.M.E. Book Concern, 1939), pp. 180–181.
19. *Ibid.,* p. 181.
20. Smith, *op. cit.,* p. 76.
21. Frazier, *op. cit.,* p. 40.
22. *The Pittsburgh Courier* (March 15, 1958), p. 3.

Chapter V

1. Smith, *op. cit.*, pp. 101–102.
2. Payne, *Recollections*, p. 217.
3. Smith, *op. cit.*, p. 113.
4. Frazier, *The Negro Church in America*, p. 43.
5. Smith, *op. cit.*, pp. 319–320.
6. Pelt and Smith, *op. cit.*, pp. 171–172.
7. Martin Luther King, Jr., *Where Do We Go From Here: Chaos or Community?* (New York, Harper & Row, Publishers, 1967), pp. 29–30.
8. Leon W. Watts II, "The National Committee of Black Churchmen," *Christianity and Crisis*, Vol. XXX, No. 18 (November 2 & 16, 1970), p. 239.
9. Frazier, *op. cit.*, p. 35.
10. August Meier, *Negro Thought in America, 1880–1915* (Ann Arbor, The University of Michigan Press, 1963), pp. 130–131.
11. Leon H. Sullivan, *Build Brother Build* (Philadelphia, Macrae Smith Company, 1969), pp. 73–74.
12. *Ibid.*, p. 76.
13. Correspondence dated April 26, 1970.
14. Correspondence dated May 12, 1970.
15. Correspondence to the author.
16. James H. Cone, "Black Consciousness and the Black Church," *Christianity and Crisis*, Vol. XXX, No. 18 (November 2 & 16, 1970), pp. 246–247.
17. Sister M. Martin De Porres Grey, "The Church, Revolution and Black Catholics," *The Black Scholar*, Vol. 2, No. 4 (December, 1970), p. 23.
18. Albert B. Cleage, Jr., *The Black Messiah* (New York, Sheed and Ward, 1968), pp. 43–44.
19. William B. McClain, "The Genius of the Black Church," *Christianity and Crisis*, Vol. XXX, No. 18 (November 2 & 16, 1970), pp. 251–252.
20. Cleage, *op. cit.*, pp. 110–111.
21. James H. Cone, *A Black Theology of Liberation* (New York, J. B. Lippincott Company, 1970), pp. 120–121, 124.
22. *Ibid.*, p. 124.
23. Thomas A. Johnson, "Black Religion Seeks Own Theology," *The New York Times* (January 20, 1971), p. 29.

Chapter VI

1. Smith, *op. cit.*, pp. 165–166.
2. Nathan Hare, "Have Negro Ministers Failed Their Roles?" *Negro Digest* (July, 1963), pp. 11–19.
3. Reverend Charles H. King, Jr., "Negro Ministers Have Not Failed—Have Sociologists?" *Negro Digest* (November, 1963), pp. 12–16.
4. Hare, *op. cit.*, p. 16.
5. "The Tragedy of an Untrained Ministry," *The Pittsburgh Courier* (October 26, 1940), p. 15.

Index